MW00784625

HORROR PUZZLES

pi

Publications International, Ltd.

Louis Weber, CEO
Publications International, Ltd.
8140 Lehigh Avenue
Morton Grove, IL 60053

ISBN: 978-1-63938-575-1

Manufactured in China.

8 7 6 5 4 3 2 1

Let's get social!

@Publications_International

@PublicationsInternational

@BrainGames.TM

www.pilbooks.com

SEARCHING FOR SOMETHING SCARY?

All work and no play can make anyone crave a mental respite. Engage your mind with a truly horrifying collection of over 150 anagrams, crosswords, cryptograms, mazes, quizzes, word searches, and more in **Brain Games® Horror Puzzles**.

Discover the actors behind your favorite iconic horror monsters, or match the obscure phobia to its ghastly definition. Navigate through accounts of real-life haunted locations, like the Winchester Mystery House in California and the Dr. Samuel A. Mudd House in Maryland, or complete the famous quotes of classic horror novels like Mary Shelley's *Frankenstein* or Henry James's *The Turn of the Screw*.

From the horrifying creatures of ancient myth that have inspired fear for thousands of years, to the point-of-view characters in your favorite horror video games, **Brain Games® Horror Puzzles** promises to deliver on some frightening fun! So lock your windows, bolt your doors, and give your brain the workout it deserves! If you need a hint, answers can be found in the back of the book.

AWFUL FEARS

Don't be afraid. There's no name for a fear of solving puzzles. Identify the meaning of each phobia.

1. AGYROPHOBIA

a.) Fear of crossing streets

b.) Fear of heavy machinery

c.) Fear of a public or crowded place

d.) Fear of silver

2. APEIROPHOBIA

a.) Fear of apes or monkeys

b.) Fear of bees or wasps

c.) Fear of deleting computer files

d.) Fear of eternity or infinity

3. ARACHIBUTYROPHOBIA

a.) Fear of the government or ruling powers

b.) Fear of opinions

c.) Fear of peanut butter sticking to the roof of your mouth

d.) Fear of spiders or spider webs

4. ATYCHIPHOBIA

a.) Fear of failure

b.) Fear of misplacing belongings

c.) Fear of public speaking

d.) Fear of rhetorical questions

LIFE AMONG THE SANE

Cryptograms are messages in substitution code. Break the code to read the quote and its author. For example, THE SMART CAT might become FVO QWGDF JGF if **F** is substituted for **T**, **V** for **H**, **O** for **E**, and so on.

"B UXVTFX BGLTGX, PBMA EHGZ

BGMXKOTEL HY AHKKBUEX LTGBMR."

—XWZTK TEETG IHX

POE ST_R__S

Below is a list of Edgar Allan Poe stories. The only thing is, they've lost **A**, **E**, **I**, **O**, **U**, and **Y**, as well as any punctuation and spaces between words. Can you figure out the missing vowels and decipher each title in the list below?

BRNC

LG

THFLLFTHHSFSHR

THMNFTHCRWD

WLLMWLSN

Answers on page 166.

GHOST STORY

Every word listed is contained within the group of letters. Words can be found in a straight line horizontally, vertically, or diagonally. They may be read either forward or backward.

BUMP	LANTERN
CHANDELIER	LIGHTNING STRIKE
CREAKY FLOOR	MOON
CURSE	PHONE CALL
DAGGER	RATTLE
DARK	SHADOWS
DOORBELL	SHRIEK
DUNGEON	SHUTTERS
EMPTY	SPIRITS
FLASHLIGHT	STORMY
GHOST	THUNDER
GHOUL	WARNING
HAUNTED HOUSE	WHISPER
HOWL	WRONG TURN

```
Y S P I R I T S H F S H R I E K
J Z Y D A R K S A L R H C C L P
D M F D T P S H U A A O H U G G
O O L U B H T A N S T W A R V H
O O A N U O O D T H T L N S T O
R N N G M N R O E L L D D E H U
B T T E P E M W D I E A E E U L
E A E O L C Y S H G L G L K N S
L X R N S A D T O H T G I J D H
L F N H F L S V U T J E E Y E U
P C G M N L J J S E A R R Q R T
C W A R N I N G E T G H O S T T
L I G H T N I N G S T R I K E E
N R H C R E A K Y F L O O R D R
T D C W H I S P E R E M P T Y S
A G B W R O N G T U R N J W M L
```

Answers on page 166.

SQUARE MAZE

Navigate the twisting path to find your way out of these endless corridors.

end

start

SAY WHAT?

Below is a group of words that, when properly arranged in the blanks, reveal a quote from Edgar Allan Poe.

DEATH LITTLE LOATHE SLEEP SLICES

" _____, those _____ _____ of _____, how I _____ them."

NORTH AMERICAN CRYPTIDS

Unscramble each word or phrase below to reveal the name of a North American cryptid.

A CAR HUBCAP

AD HOG

AFTER CLOWN HERRINGS (two words)

ALASKAN FELTED MOTHER (three words)

BEST BOA FOCUS (three words)

CLOAK JAPE

DOME VENDOR (two words)

DRY EELS JIVE (two words)

FIG BOOT

FLOATED SNOWSTORM (two words)

Answers on page 166 & 167.

DEATH'S HOUSE

Cryptograms are messages in substitution code. Break the code to read the message. For example, THE SMART CAT might become FVO QWGDF JGF if **F** is substituted for **T**, **V** for **H**, **O** for **E**, and so on.

"TXF, UXOCJ. UXOCJ LWFC YX FR
YXOWCSKWZ. CR ZSX SQ CJX FRKC YIRNQ
XOICJ, NSCJ CJX PIOFFXF NOHSQP OYRHX
RQX'F JXOU, OQU ZSFCXQ CR FSZXQVX. CR
JOHX QR TXFCXIUOT, OQU QR CR-LRIIRN.
CR KRIPXC CSLX, CR KRIPXC ZSKX, CR YX
OC BXOVX. TRW VOQ JXZB LX. TRW VOQ
RBXQ KRI LX CJX BRICOZF RK UXOCJ'F
JRWFX, KRI ZRHX SF OZNOTF NSCJ TRW,
OQU ZRHX SF FCIRQPXI CJOQ UXOCJ SF."
—RFVOI NSZUX, CJX VOQCXIHSZZX PJRFC

FOND DU LAC GHOSTS (PART I)

(Read this haunted account, then turn to the next page to test your knowledge.)

Listed on the National Register of Historic places, the Ramada Plaza Hotel in Fond du Lac, Wisconsin, is also on more than one "most haunted" list. Built in the 1920s, this structure was originally known as the Hotel Retlaw, after owner Walter Schroeder. ("Retlaw" is "Walter" spelled backward.) And even though Walter is no longer alive, he appears to have remained at his namesake hotel.

In its heyday, this eight-story building was one of the premier hotels in Wisconsin along with several others that were owned by Schroeder. Located at the junction of four major Wisconsin highways, the inn attracted some prominent guests, such as John F. Kennedy, Eleanor Roosevelt, Hubert Humphrey, and numerous Wisconsin politicians. Over the years, there have been so many stories of ghosts at the hotel that employees started keeping a log to record the activity. Some say that Walter Schroeder was murdered there and that it's his ghost that haunts the property. But it seems that he's not alone.

The most haunted area of the hotel is Room 717, where visitors and staff have heard screams and other noises—all while the room is empty. Faucets and lights turn themselves on and off, and the TV changes stations on its own—this ghost seems to favor C-SPAN.

Other paranormal activity has been observed throughout the hotel. Strange humming when no one is around, a ghostly figure walking into walls, and an odd glow in the banquet room are all part of the fun. One frequently seen apparition is a redheaded woman in a white bathrobe; she disappears into the wall when startled. In addition, the chandelier in the ballroom sometimes sways for no reason, and an employee spotted a couple dancing there. He thought it was rather sweet... until the pair vanished.

On a side note, it was believed that the ghost of Walter Schroeder also haunted the Retlaw Theater, which was located just a block away from the hotel. Coincidence? Probably not.

FOND DU LAC GHOSTS (PART II)

(Do not read this until you have read the previous page!)

1. What was the original name of the Ramada Plaza Hotel?

    A. Hotel Jigsaw

    B. Hotel Outlaw

    C. Hotel Retlaw

    D. Hotel Retan

2. How many stories does the structure have?

    A. 8

    B. 10

    C. 12

    D. 14

3. Which of the following people was not a guest at the Ramada Plaza?

    A. Eleanor Roosevelt

    B. Elvis Presley

    C. Hubert Humphrey

    D. John F. Kennedy

4. Which is the hotel's most haunted room?

    A. 117

    B. 707

    C. 711

    D. 717

HAUNTED HOTEL

A ghost haunts one of the 45 hotel rooms listed in the chart below. A team of paranormal investigators received a list of four cryptic clues from a hotline caller reporting the sighting. Using these clues, the paranormal investigators found the room number—but by that time, the ghost had vanished. Can you find the haunted hotel room more quickly?

1. The first digit is smaller than the second.

2. Neither digit is 3 or 4.

3. However, the number is divisible by 4.

4. The sum of the digits is more than 10.

51	52	53	54	55	56	57	58	59
41	42	43	44	45	46	47	48	49
31	32	33	34	35	36	37	38	39
21	22	23	24	25	26	27	28	29
11	12	13	14	15	16	17	18	19

Answer on page 167.

BEST-SELLING HORROR NOVELS

Place these horror novels in chronological order from earliest to latest.

1.

2.

3.

4.

5.

6.

7.

8.

9.

10.

A. *Dracula*

B. *The Exorcist*

C. *Flowers in the Attic*

D. *Frankenstein*

E. *The Haunting of Hill House*

F. *It*

G. *Pet Sematary*

H. *Ring*

I. *The Shining*

J. *The Silence of the Lambs*

CIRCLE MAZE

Navigate the circular labyrinth to escape the monster.

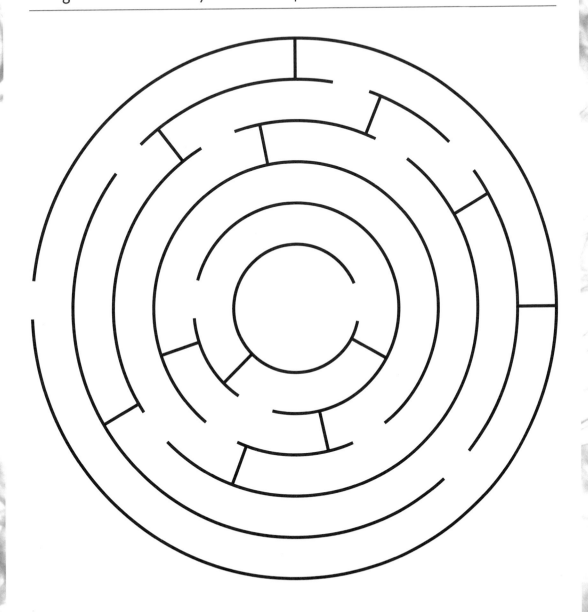

Answer on page 167.

THE HAUNTED ALCATRAZ ISLAND

At times a military fort, a maximum-security prison, and the site of a months-long Native American protest, Alcatraz Island has a complex history. Now managed by the National Park Service, this island in San Francisco Bay is open to tours. As the former home to some of the most notorious criminals in history, including Al Capone and Arthur "Doc" Barker, it's no wonder that Alcatraz is considered one of the most haunted places in the nation. Voices, screams, sobs, and clanging doors are sometimes heard, and guests have even reported seeing an "entity" with glowing red eyes.

ALCATRAZ ISLAND

CALIFORNIA

FEDERAL PENITENTIARY

GHOSTS

HAUNTED

HISTORICAL

INMATES

ISLAND

LA ISLA DE LOS (Alcatraces)

LIGHTHOUSE

MAXIMUM-SECURITY (Prison)

MILITARY FORT

MOST-HAUNTED
(in the nation, possibly)

NATIVE AMERICANS

PHANTOM SCREAMS

PROTESTS

RED-EYED ENTITY

SAN FRANCISCO

SAN FRANCISCO BAY

THE ISLAND OF THE
(Pelicans)

TOURIST ATTRACTION

```
G O J O C L Y T I T N E D E Y E D E R T
T J F S A N F R A N C I S C O B A Y C N
F E D E R A L P E N I T E N T I A R Y O
N I E C D E T N U A H T S O M Y Z E A I
D A H U M L A I S L A D E L O S J F D T
W H T H Y A B N G C A I N R O F I L A C
S T D I X B X S S S T W U U Z G O T R A
M B R N V Y S I T A E V Z H O H L H N R
A K U O A E T P M S C T V O N O W E L T
E L R D F L A I D U E H A T P S U I I T
R A G F N Y S M L H M T Q M G T G S G A
C C Q U B L R I E G H S O P N S K L H T
S I Y U A S W A Z R G A E R I I V A T S
M R P N A F Z N T A I G U C P U V N H I
O O D B E Z S P P I R C G N U E K D O R
T T A Q Z B E F G N L T A F T R R O U U
N S H U I I B Y I M Y I A N Q E I F S O
A I N W T Q P X H X L B M C S A D T E T
H H Q E G V I O D K R L O U L X R H Y P
P O C S I C N A R F N A S E W A G E X E
```

Answers on page 168.

MEND THE BRIDGES

A rampaging monster has barreled through the entire county, destroying all the bridges indicated by circles. Your job is to travel to each location—A through I, in any order—by restoring only 2 of the bridges.

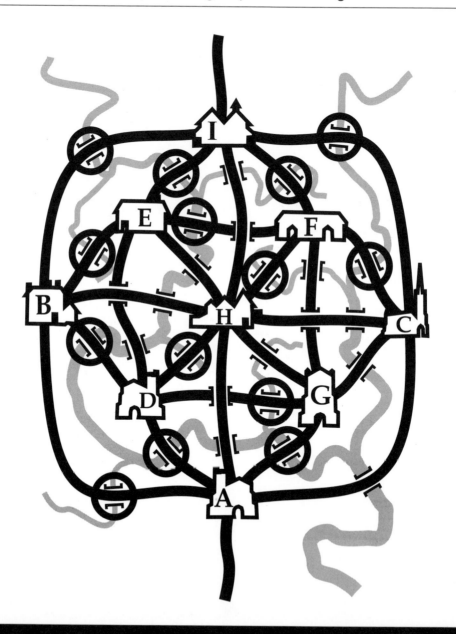

MORE NORTH AMERICAN CRYPTIDS

Unscramble each word or phrase below to reveal the name of a North American cryptid.

CAT SQUASH

COMPLETION PERKS
(three words)

ENTWINED SALESMEN
(two words)

GLASSY RENTAL

HAWK RINK SAUNA (two words)

KEA SPUNK (two words)

MUSCAT PAW (two words)

THAN MOM

VERNAL ALMOND FOG
(two words)

WIG UP DUKE

H_RR_R G_NR_S

Below is a list of horror genres. The only thing is, they've lost **A, E, I, O, U,** and **Y,** as well as any punctuation and spaces between words. Can you figure out the missing vowels and decipher each genre in the list below?

B D

C M D C

C R M

D M N C P S S S S N

P C L P T C

Answers on page 168.

BONE-CHILLING FEARS

Don't be afraid. There's no name for a fear of solving puzzles. Identify the meaning of each phobia.

---

1. BASOPHOBIA

a.) Fear of blood

b.) Fear of driving

c.) Fear of falling

d.) Fear of reptiles

2. BATRACHOPHOBIA

a.) Fear of amphibians

b.) Fear of bathing or washing

c.) Fear of bats

d.) Fear of night

3. BELONEPHOBIA

a.) Fear of being forgotten

b.) Fear of the color white

c.) Fear of cooked or raw meats

d.) Fear of sharp or pointed objects

4. BIBLIOPHOBIA

a.) Fear of books or reading

b.) Fear of long words

c.) Fear of paper

d.) Fear of school

Answers on page 168.

MORBID MUSE

Cryptograms are messages in substitution code. Break the code to read the quote and its author. For example, THE SMART CAT might become FVO QWGDF JGF if **F** is substituted for **T**, **V** for **H**, **O** for **E**, and so on.

"OCZ YZVOC OCZI JA V WZVPODAPG RJHVI

DN PILPZNODJIVWGT OCZ HJNO KJZODXVG

OJKDX DI OCZ RJMGY, VIY ZLPVGGT DN DO

WZTJIY YJPWO OCVO OCZ GDKN WZNO

NPDOZY AJM NPXC OJKDX VMZ OCJNZ JA V

WZMZVQZY GJQZM." —ZYBVM VGGVI KJZ

POE P__MS

Below is a list of Edgar Allan Poe poems. The only thing is, they've lost **A**, **E**, **I**, **O**, **U**, and **Y**, as well as any punctuation and spaces between words. Can you figure out th`e missing vowels and decipher each title in the list below?

DRMWTHNDRM

LNR

NNBLL

THBLLS

THRVN

GHOSTS OF LITERATURE

Match these famous ghosts of literature to their original stories.

1. Akaky Akakievich Bashmachkin

2. Banquo

3. The Bleeding Nun

4. The Headless Horseman

5. Jacob Marley

6. King Hamlet

7. Lady Rowena

8. Peter Quint

9. The Seafaring Spirit

10. Sir Simon

A. William Shakespeare, *Hamlet* (~1603)

B. William Shakespeare, *Macbeth* (1606)

C. Matthew Lewis, *The Monk* (1796)

D. Washington Irving, "The Legend of Sleepy Hollow" (1820)

E. Edgar Allan Poe, "Ligeia" (1838)

F. Nikolai Gogol, "The Overcoat" (1842)

G. Charles Dickens, *A Christmas Carol* (1843)

H. F. Marion Crawford, "The Upper Berth" (1886)

I. Oscar Wilde, "The Canterville Ghost" (1887)

J. Henry James, *The Turn of the Screw* (1898)

HAUNTED HOTEL

A ghost haunts one of the 45 hotel rooms listed in the chart below. A team of paranormal investigators received a list of four cryptic clues from a hotline caller reporting the sighting. Using these clues, the paranormal investigators found the room number—but by that time, the ghost had vanished. Can you find the haunted hotel room more quickly?

1. Both digits are odd numbers.

2. The first digit is less than the second digit.

3. The sum of the digits is 8 or less.

4. It is divisible by 5 and 7.

51	52	53	54	55	56	57	58	59
41	42	43	44	45	46	47	48	49
31	32	33	34	35	36	37	38	39
21	22	23	24	25	26	27	28	29
11	12	13	14	15	16	17	18	19

Answer on page 169.

SAY BOO

ACROSS

1. Talon
5. Bass ____
11. It's pumped at the pumps
14. Ethiopian of opera
15. Priced to move
16. Web site address: abbr.
17. Haunted house opener?
19. What Pan never did
20. Edison rival Nikola
21. Nonalcoholic brew
22. December deposit
23. Former Davis Cup captain
26. Carries a lot of weight
28. Without delay
33. Santa ____ (hot winds)
34. Bering, for one: abbr.
35. Composition for 9
37. "Blimey!"
38. Putting into circulation
41. A year in Dali's life
42. ____ renewal
44. Late opening?
45. Rank below Capt.
46. Ceased to exist
50. Quebec peninsula
51. "Hairy man" in Genesis 27:11
52. Something to slip on
54. Roadwork sign
56. Lucy's neighbor
60. And others; abbr.
61. Medicinal flowering plants
64. Geneticist's abbr.
65. One-named folk singer
66. City with a leaning tower
67. Ahn's "Kung Fu" role
68. Got up again
69. Smell ____

DOWN

1. Wield a fly rod
2. Be partial to
3. Dog-days drinks
4. Workers, in India
5. Learned
6. Tres minus dos
7. "____ that something!"
8. Cue for a drum solo
9. On ____ (tethered)
10. Spanish monarch
11. Naval base much in the news
12. Golden Fleece carrier
13. A lot
18. Direction
22. Chris of baseball
24. Little Joe's brother
25. Small salamanders
27. ____ shui (Chinese study)
28. "That's Italian!" sauce
29. Like many chemical compounds: abbr.
30. Dumpster's little brother
31. Cocktail
32. Keeps an eye on
36. Reform
38. Hero endings
39. "____ for real?"
40. Turndowns
43. Grandfatherly
45. Pluck
47. Positive aspect
48. One who throws stones

Answers on page 169.

49. Titan matriarch
52. Buoy (with "up")
53. Valle del Bove setting
55. Numerical prefix
57. Junior, to Senior's estate

58. Lanchester of films
59. Future lawyer's exam: abbr.
61. NYC superstation
62. Atlas abbr.
63. Own, to a Scot

SAY WHAT?

Below is a group of words that, when properly arranged in the blanks, reveal a quote from *The Monk* by Matthew Gregory Lewis.

ACQUIRE   DESTINY   FRIEND   RESTLESSNESS   WORLD

"I have no _____ in the _____, and from the _____ of

my _____ I never can _____ one."

SHIRLEY JACKSON H_RR_R

Below is a list of Shirley Jackson stories. The only thing is, they've lost **A**, **E**, **I**, **O**, **U**, and **Y**, as well as any punctuation and spaces between words. Can you figure out the missing vowels and decipher each title in the list below?

H N G S M N

T H B R D S N S T

T H H N T N G F H L L H S

T H L T T R

T H S N D L

CONVENIENT HOUSE

Cryptograms are messages in substitution code. Break the code to read the message. For example, THE SMART CAT might become FVO QWGDF JGF if **F** is substituted for **T**, **V** for **H**, **O** for **E**, and so on.

"D PIJ EPM YDMB QX I ZITENM QX

HQAIFZM DFPICDEMJ CR I HQTR TVHDEM,

TKZP I VNIZM IT BQKNJ TQAMPQB, XQH

JDYMHTDQF QX EPM RQKFW DJMI, EISM

INN ZQNQH QKE QX TEQHRCQQST IFJ

XIDHREINMT. BITF'E DE OKTE I

TEQHRCQQS QYMH BPDZP D PIJ XINNMF

IJQLM IFJ IJHMIA? FQ; DE BIT I CDW,

KWNR, IFEDGKM, CKE ZQFYMFDMFE

PQKTM, MACQJRDFW I XMB XMIEKHMT QX

I CKDNJDFW TEDNN QNJMH, PINX-

HMVNIZMJ IFJ PINX-KEDNDLMJ, DF BPDZP

D PIJ EPM XIFZR QX QKH CMDFW INAQTE

IT NQTE IT I PIFJXKN QX VITTMFWMHT DF

I WHMIE JHDXEDFW TPDV. BMNN, D BIT,

TEHIFWMNR, IE EPM PMNA!" —PMFHR

OIAMT, EPM EKHF QX EPM TZHMB

MORE GHOSTS OF LITERATURE

Match these famous ghosts of literature to their original stories.

1. Damiana Cisneros

2. The Dead Men of Dunharrow

3. The Grady Sisters

4. Jennet Humfrye

5. Michael Furey

6. Mrs. Owens

7. The Reverend Everly Thomas

8. Sara Tidwell

9. Susie Salmon

10. William Ager

A. James Joyce, "The Dead" (1914)

B. M.R. James, "A Warning to the Curious" (1925)

C. J.R.R. Tolkien, *The Lord of the Rings* (1954)

D. Juan Rulfo, *Pedro Parámo* (1955)

E. Stephen King, *The Shining* (1977)

F. Susan Hill, *The Woman in Black* (1983)

G. Stephen King, *Bag of Bones* (1998)

H. Alice Sebold, *The Lovely Bones* (2002)

I. Neil Gaiman, *The Graveyard Book* (2008)

J. George Saunders, *Lincoln in the Bardo* (2017)

SQUARE MAZE

Navigate the twisting path to find your way out of these endless corridors.

start

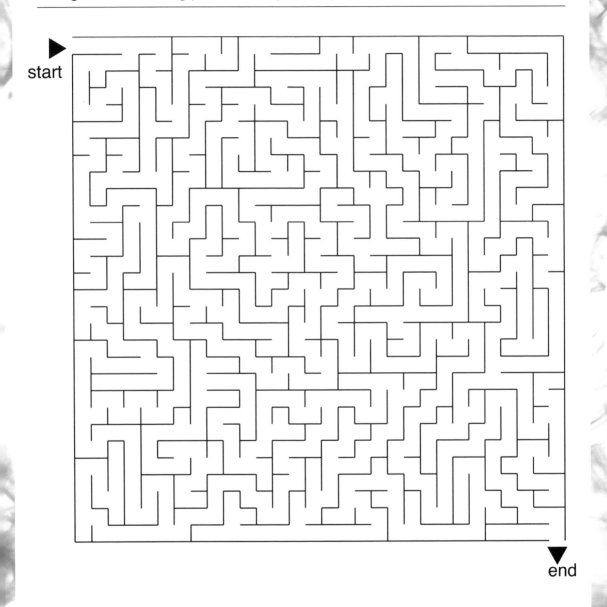

end

Answer on page 170.

MEND THE BRIDGES

A rampaging monster has barreled through the entire county, destroying all the bridges indicated by circles. Your job is to travel to each location—A through I, in any order—by restoring only 2 of the bridges.

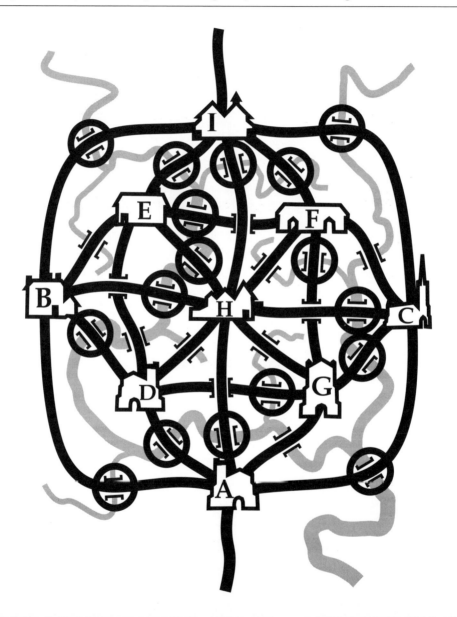

CREEPY FEARS

Don't be afraid. There's no name for a fear of solving puzzles. Identify the meaning of each phobia.

1. CACOPHOBIA

a.) Fear of being unhappy

b.) Fear of injury

c.) Fear of loud noises

d.) Fear of ugliness

2. CHEROPHOBIA

a.) Fear of bad weather

b.) Fear of cherries

c.) Fear of dancing

d.) Fear of happiness

3. CHROMOPHOBIA

a.) Fear of chrome

b.) Fear of colors

c.) Fear of metronomes

d.) Fear of time

4. COIMETROPHOBIA

a.) Fear of being stared at

b.) Fear of cemeteries

c.) Fear of group projects

d.) Fear of styled hair

Answers on page 170.

H_RR_R G_NR_S

Below is a list of horror genres. The only thing is, they've lost **A**, **E**, **I**, **O**, **U**, and **Y**, as well as any punctuation and spaces between words. Can you figure out the missing vowels and decipher each genre in the list below?

FLK

FNDFTG

GTHC

HNTDHS

LVCRFTN

HATRED

Cryptograms are messages in substitution code. Break the code to read the message. For example, THE SMART CAT might become FVO QWGDF JGF if **F** is substituted for **T**, **V** for **H**, **O** for **E**, and so on.

"A RAUU PNHNTEN SF ATLXPANM: AV A QDTTYI ATMGAPN UYHN, A RAUU QDXMN VNDP; DTJ QOANVUF IYRDPJM FYX SF DPQO-NTNSF, KNQDXMN SF QPNDIYP, JY A MRNDP ATNZIATEXAMODKUN ODIPNJ."
—SDPF MONUUNF, VPDTWNTMINAT

SQUARE MAZE

Navigate the twisting path to find your way out of these endless corridors.

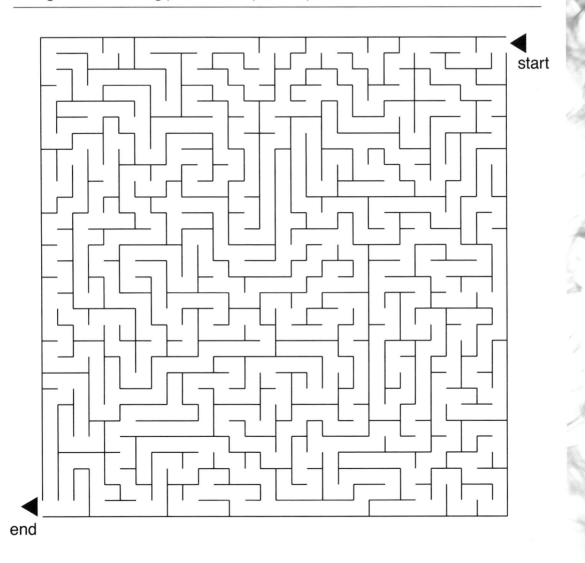

start

end

Answer on page 171.

FRANKENSTEIN

ARCTIC

CLERVAL

COTTAGE

CREATURE

ELIZABETH

EPISTOLARY

FATHER

FRANKENSTEIN

GALVANISM

GENEVA

GROUNDBREAKING

HORROR

JUSTINE

MARY SHELLEY

ORKNEY

PROMETHEUS

SCIENTIST

SWITZERLAND

VICTOR

WALTON

```
D E N E N I T S U J T S F L D P
G P B I O D W X V A C N M C F N
N L R S E Q A I C I O S R M W K
I G H O J T C E E I I B A F C G
K F T H M T S N G N T R A Z L O
A J E K O E T N A A Y C X X E R
E J B R Z I T V E S T C R S R K
R K A I S J L H H K G T H A V N
B P Z T P A J E E W N E O I A E
D R I A G W L V A U I A N C L Y
N E L X Z L O L D S S H R E N J
U H E H E Q T H O R R O R F V J
O T T Y O O C R K A Z G S L H A
R A M D N A L R E Z T I W S Q T
G F I W J E G U C R E A T U R E
K M G R E P I S T O L A R Y X C
```

Answers on page 171.

MEXICAN MONSTERS

Unscramble each word or phrase below to reveal a creature of Mexican folklore.

A CHUTE UPHILL

A ROLL LOAN (two words)

AN CHEQUE

CACTI LIP

ION TOTAL

LAGUNA

MORON REBELS (two words)

NAN DUCT DUNT

UNREALIZED DOLL (four words)

VIA COY HAW (two words)

SAY WHAT?

Below is a group of words that, when properly arranged in the blanks, reveal a quote from *Frankenstein* by Mary Shelley.

ESCAPE INDULGE LOVE ONE RAGE SATISFIED SEEN

"There is _____ in me the likes of which you've never _____.

There is _____ in me the likes of which should never _____.

If I am not _____ in the _____, I will _____ the other."

THY CREATURE

Cryptograms are messages in substitution code. Break the code to read the message. For example, THE SMART CAT might become FVO QWGDF JGF if **F** is substituted for **T**, **V** for **H**, **O** for **E**, and so on.

"U SP BIM OLYSBTLY, SQE U FUWW CY YAYQ PUWE SQE EHOUWY BH PM QSBTLSW WHLE SQE RUQX, UK BIHT FUWB SWVH JYLKHLP BIM JSLB, BIY FIUOI BIHT HFYVB PY. HI, KLSQRYQVBYUQ, CY QHB YGTUBSCWY BH YAYLM HBIYL, SQE BLSPJWY TJHQ PY SWHQY, BH FIHP BIM DTVBUOY, SQE YAYQ BIM OWYPYQOM SQE SKKYOBUHQ, UV PHVB ETY. LYPYPCYL, BISB U SP BIM OLYSBTLY: U HTXIB BH CY BIM SESP; CTB U SP LSBIYL BIY KSWWYQ SQXYW, FIHP BIHT ELUAYVB KLHP DHM KHL QH PUVEYYE. YAYLM FIYLY U VYY CWUVV, KLHP FIUOI U SWHQY SP ULLYAHOSCWM YZOWTEYE. U FSV CYQYAHWYQB SQE XHHE; PUVYLM PSEY PY S KUYQE. PSRY PY ISJJM, SQE U VISWW SXSUQ CY AULBTHTV." —PSLM VIYWWYM, KLSQRYQVBYUQ

Answers on page 171.

HAUNTED HOTEL

A ghost haunts one of the 45 hotel rooms listed in the chart below. A team of paranormal investigators received a list of four cryptic clues from a hotline caller reporting the sighting. Using these clues, the paranormal investigators found the room number—but by that time, the ghost had vanished. Can you find the haunted hotel room more quickly?

1. The number cannot be divided evenly by 5.

2. The number can be divided by 3.

3. If you add the digits together, the result is greater than 6.

4. If you reversed the digits, the resulting number would be found on the chart.

51	52	53	54	55	56	57	58	59
41	42	43	44	45	46	47	48	49
31	32	33	34	35	36	37	38	39
21	22	23	24	25	26	27	28	29
11	12	13	14	15	16	17	18	19

HAUNTED CATFISH PLANTATION (PART I)

(Read this haunted account, then turn to the next page to test your knowledge.)

Fort Worth Paranormal once deemed the Catfish Plantation in Waxahachie, Texas, "one of the most haunted restaurants in the entire country." With several spirits in residence, this Victorian building lives up to that designation.

As is the case at many haunted places, this restaurant has cold spots, doors that lock and unlock by themselves, water faucets and lights that turn on and off without human intervention, and refrigerator doors that open and close on their own. In addition, a number of dinner knives mysteriously come up missing every night. Perhaps some of this is the doing of the restaurant's three resident ghosts.

The quietest spirit is that of Will, a farmer who died of pneumonia when he lived in the building in the 1930s; he's been seen loitering on the front porch. It is believed that he is responsible for some of the cold spots. He's typically very shy, but he has been known to touch women's legs while they're eating.

A more active ghost is that of Elizabeth Anderson, a young woman who lived in the building until the early 1920s, when a former boyfriend murdered her on the day that she was supposed to marry another man. Her appearances are preceded by the scent of roses. Elizabeth is sometimes seen in the bay window in the front room. Once, she even followed a customer home and presented her with an antique powder box as a gift.

A third spirit that resides at the Catfish Plantation is believed to be that of a woman named Caroline, who died in the building in the 1970s at age 80. Although no one has actually seen her ghost, her presence is deeply felt, and she wants to remind everyone that the building is still her home. When the restaurant opened in 1984, Caroline greeted the new owner with a pot of freshly brewed coffee. Another time, the owner was surprised to discover a large tea urn positioned in the middle of the kitchen floor; all the cups were stacked neatly inside it. Caroline has also been known to throw coffee cups, wineglasses, spices, and food.

HAUNTED CATFISH PLANTATION (PART II)

(Do not read this until you have read the previous page!)

1. Which of the following types of tableware goes missing every night?

    A. Bread plates

    B. Forks

    C. Knives

    D. Napkins

2. Farmer Will, the quietest spirit on the Catfish Plantation, succumbed to pneumonia.

    _____ True

    _____ False

3. What is the name of the most active spirit?

    A. Caroline

    B. Elizabeth

    C. Nancy

    D. Sophia

4. What was the restaurant owner surprised to see on the floor?

    A. Pot of coffee

    B. Salt shaker

    C. Tea urn

    D. Wineglass

HORROR NOVELS

Match each author to the horror novel they wrote.

---

1. Daphne du Maurier

2. Jeremias Gotthelf

3. Shirley Jackson

4. Henry James

5. Joseph Sheridan Le Fanu

6. H.P. Lovecraft

7. William March

8. Richard Matheson

9. Mary Shelley

10. Bram Stoker

A. *Frankenstein* (1818)

B. *The Black Spider* (1842)

C. *Carmilla* (1872)

D. *Dracula* (1897)

E. *The Turn of the Screw* (1898)

F. *At the Mountains of Madness* (1936)

G. *Rebecca* (1938)

H. *The Bad Seed* (1954)

I. *I Am Legend* (1954)

J. *The Haunting of Hill House* (1959)

Answers on page 172.

THE HAUNTED ALLEN HOUSE

Arkansas businessman Joe Lee Allen lived in his 1900s Queen-Anne home in Monticello, Arkansas, until his death in 1917. Joe Lee Allen died of a heart attack at the age of 54. In the late 1940s, Allen's daughter, LaDell Allen, died in the house after consuming cyanide. The room where LaDell died was sealed off for nearly 40 years. The house was later turned into apartments; the apartment tenants subsequently reported hearing unusual sounds and seeing shadowy figures.

APARTMENTS

ARKANSAS

BUSINESSMAN

CADDYE ALLEN (Mother)

CYANIDE

DEVELOPED

DIED

FAMILY HOME

HAUNTED

HEART ATTACK

JOE LEE ALLEN (Father)

LADELL ALLEN (Daughter)

LEWIE ALLEN (Daughter)

LONNIE ALLEN (Daughter)

MANSION

MONTICELLO

PARANORMAL

QUEEN ANNE STYLE

REST IN PEACE

SHADOWY FIGURES

SUICIDE

THE OLD ALLEN HOUSE

UNUSUAL SOUNDS

```
E D C A D D Y E A L L E N O O J M B A K
L A E C A E P N I T S E R A U C M I Z S
Y R O E Q L A D E L L A L L E N V N W U
T W W X T S D N U O S L A U S U N U W I
S J Z Z B P R U D O L L E C I T N O M C
E Z X D R W L E W I E A L L E N F E T I
N O O E U S E R K D E D I N A Y C E Y D
N U I I D H F A M I L Y H O M E Y F F E
A J M D E A N P A R M A M T T H V I I I
N O V T V D E J P S A X O A T Y K O H N
E E T H E O L D A L L E N H O U S E A L
E L O J L W L A R X E N T P W H A M I Y
U E S T O Y A E T G G T T L A R S R N E
Q E A P P F E C M T N Q K U T S O O H A
R A S R E I I T E D W X N A E N I N A M
Q L N T D G N B N Z B T T N L S N J I S
D L A K W U N C T C E T I K N P H G K E
C E K T Z R O Z S D A S J A K K D Y Y Z
V N R R U E L O X C U B M M Q V H Q T G
J Y A P T S H Y K B P A R A N O R M A L
```

Answers on page 172.

CROSSOVER MAZE

Cross over and under tunnels to reach the end of the underground lair.

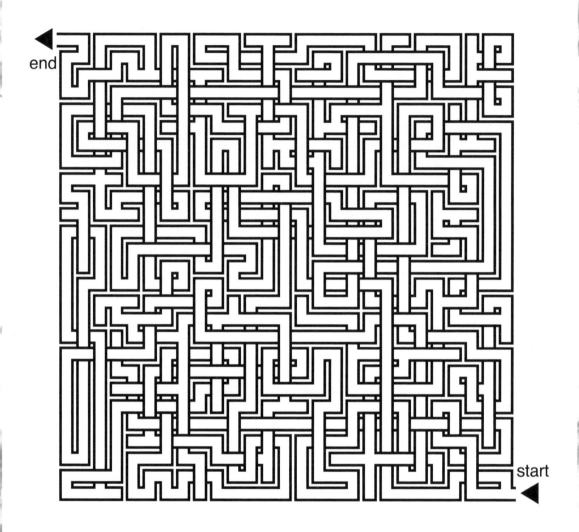

end

start

MEND THE BRIDGES

A rampaging monster has barreled through the entire county, destroying all the bridges indicated by circles. Your job is to travel to each location—A through I, in any order—by restoring only 2 of the bridges.

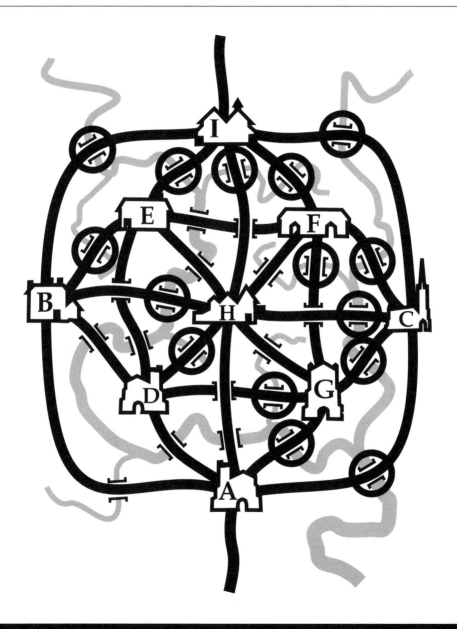

Answer on page 172.

CELTIC MONSTERS

Unscramble each word or phrase below to reveal a creature of Celtic folklore.

A BATH ARCH

CHAPEL RUNE

DEAD URGE (two words)

EEL SKI

ELK PIE

FAIR MOONS

HAS BEEN

HULA LAND

LAUGHS

LEND LEECH RENT
(two words)

POE ST_R__S

Below is a list of Edgar Allan Poe stories. The only thing is, they've lost **A**, **E, I, O, U**, and **Y**, as well as any punctuation and spaces between words. Can you figure out the missing vowels and decipher each title in the list below?

THCSKFMNTLLD

THGLDBG

THEPRLNDLTTR

THPRMTRBRL

THTLLTLHRT

EERIE FEARS

Don't be afraid. There's no name for a fear of solving puzzles. Identify the meaning of each phobia.

1. EISOPTROPHOBIA

a.) Fear of the color yellow

b.) Fear of mirrors

c.) Fear of ophthalmologists

d.) Fear of still water

2. ENOCHLOPHOBIA

a.) Fear of alcohol

b.) Fear of crowds

c.) Fear of dates and times

d.) Fear of large animals

3. EPHEBIPHOBIA

a.) Fear of being scared

b.) Fear of eternity or infinity

c.) Fear of soldiers

d.) Fear of youth

4. ERYTHROPHOBIA

a.) Fear of blood

b.) Fear of the color red

c.) Fear of congestion or mucus

d.) Fear of extreme temperatures

Answers on page 173.

MORE HORROR NOVELS

Match each author to the horror novel they wrote.

1. Clive Barker

2. Robert Bloch

3. Ray Bradbury

4. James Herbert

5. Susan Hill

6. Stephen King

7. Ira Levin

8. Anne Rice

9. Ray Russell

10. Peter Straub

A. *Psycho* (1959)

B. *The Case Against Satan* (1962)

C. *Something Wicked This Way Comes* (1962)

D. *Rosemary's Baby* (1967)

E. *The Rats* (1974)

F. *Interview with the Vampire* (1976)

G. *The Shining* (1977)

H. *Ghost Story* (1979)

I. *The Woman in Black* (1983)

J. *Books of Blood* (1984)

H_RR_R G_NR_S

Below is a list of horror genres. The only thing is, they've lost **A, E, I, O, U**, and **Y**, as well as any punctuation and spaces between words. Can you figure out the missing vowels and decipher each genre in the list below?

MNSTR

PRNRML

PSCHLGCL

SCNCFCTN

SLSHR

SPIDER

Cryptograms are messages in substitution code. Break the code to read the message. For example, THE SMART CAT might become FVO QWGDF JGF if **F** is substituted for **T**, **V** for **H**, **O** for **E**, and so on.

"JGD TCYDY PYISYJ OTYIIL, WCY LXSOYD ZVK BGW LWSD, BYSWCYD PK OVK BGD PK BSUCW." —EYDYZSVL UGWWCYIJ, WCY PIVRM LXSOYD

MASTER OF SUSPENSE

ACROSS

1. Trumpet, for one
5. Bronze, e.g.
10. First: abbr.
14. Slurpee rival
15. Covent Garden architect Jones
16. Detective Wolfe
17. 1938 thriller starring Margaret Lockwood
20. Square of turf
21. Dies _____ (Latin hymn)
22. Metamorphic rock
23. CBS forensics drama
24. State sch. in Tucson
25. 1945 Ingrid Bergman/Gregory Peck thriller
30. The m in E=mc
34. Contend
35. Lost traction
36. All _____ up (agitated)
37. Tiresome one
38. Concert pianist André
39. A few bucks?
40. Nice summer
41. Beanstalk giant, e.g.
42. Sporty car
43. College mil. offering
45. 1954 James Stewart/Grace Kelly thriller
47. Bookie's numbers
49. Suffix with sulf-
50. Like some escapes
53. Shake _____
55. Duffel
58. 1947 courtroom drama starring Gregory Peck
61. Afflictions
62. Love, Italian-style
63. Sports cable channel
64. Little fella
65. Beeper
66. For fear that

DOWN

1. Top 40 songs
2. Eight, in Ecuador
3. Singer Lou
4. "_____ Blu, Dipinto Di Blu"
5. Central vein of a leaf
6. One-named Irish singer
7. Seedy bar
8. Khan title
9. Unfavorable probability
10. Pants measurement
11. Classic soft drink
12. Makes mad
13. Deep-six
18. Wedding walkway
19. Army div.
23. These very words
24. Person who brings others together
25. Fencing sword
26. Type starter
27. Everglades wader
28. Oil-rich Indians
29. To-the-max prefix
31. Out in front
32. Take care of
33. "That's the last _____!"
38. Text-editing feature
39. Take a meal
42. Winged nuisance
44. Body of mysteries
46. Frankfurter
48. Dennis Quaid movie
50. Cereal box stat
51. Sailor's call

52. Smell to high heaven
53. Work like _____
54. Milano moola, once
55. Foundation

56. Nile reptiles
57. Lady's man
59. Doc bloc
60. Animation frame

Answers on page 174.

SAY WHAT?

Below is a group of words that, when properly arranged in the blanks, reveal a quote from George A. Romero.

ALWAYS HORROR NEIGHBORS NEXT

REAL SCARIEST THAT

"I've _____ felt that the _____ _____ is _____ door to us,

_____ the _____ monsters are our _____."

POE ST_R__S

Below is a list of Edgar Allan Poe stories. The only thing is, they've lost **A, E, I, O, U,** and **Y**, as well as any punctuation and spaces between words. Can you figure out the missing vowels and decipher each title in the list below?

THBLCKCT

THMRDRSNTHRMRG

THMSQFTHRDDTH

THPTNDTHPNDLM

THVLPRTRT

MAD WITH LOVE

Cryptograms are messages in substitution code. Break the code to read the message. For example, THE SMART CAT might become FVO QWGDF JGF if **F** is substituted for **T**, **V** for **H**, **O** for **E**, and so on.

"ORNH GRUQCOQHN XLPN MLD OJ
TNLU. CRN OUNYZKNB KNCO NUQV
CRJWKB BQCGJPNU MRNUN ULJWK MLC
RQBBNH; CRN OJKB WC QH L TNM
RWUUQNB MJUBC ORLO NUQV RLB
XJHN IWQON YLB MQOR KJPN LHB ORLO
RN RLB BNGQBNB OJ VQKK NPNUDZJBD
LHB RQYCNKT MQOR NPNUDZJBD QT
CRN BQB HJO GJHCNHO OJ ZNGJYN
RQC MQTN. RN RLB XQPNH RNU OQKK
NKNPNH J'GKJGV ORN HNAO NPNHQHX
TJU UNTKNGOQJH. QO MLC ORN KLCO
UNCFQON. CRN YWCO GRJJCN, LC RN
CLQB, ZNOMNNH ORN MNBBQHX YLCC
LHB ORN UNIWQNY." —XLCOJH KNUJWA,
ORN FRLHOJY JT ORN JFNUL

EVEN MORE HORROR NOVELS

Match each author to the horror novel they wrote.

1. Octavia E. Butler

2. Mark Z. Danielewsi

3. Glen Duncan

4. Thomas Harris

5. Stephen King

6. Dean Koontz

7. Toni Morrison

8. Dan Simmons

9. Koji Suzuki

10. Chang Yu-ko

A. *IT* (1986)

B. *Beloved* (1987)

C. *The Silence of the Lambs* (1988)

D. *Ring* (1991)

E. *House of Leaves* (2000)

F. *The Taking* (2004)

G. *Fledgling* (2005)

H. *The Terror* (2007)

I. *The Last Werewolf* (2011)

J. *Whisper* (2018)

SQUARE MAZE

Navigate the twisting path to find your way out of these endless corridors.

start

end

Answer on page 174.

MEND THE BRIDGES

A rampaging monster has barreled through the entire county, destroying all the bridges indicated by circles. Your job is to travel to each location—A through I, in any order—by restoring only 2 of the bridges.

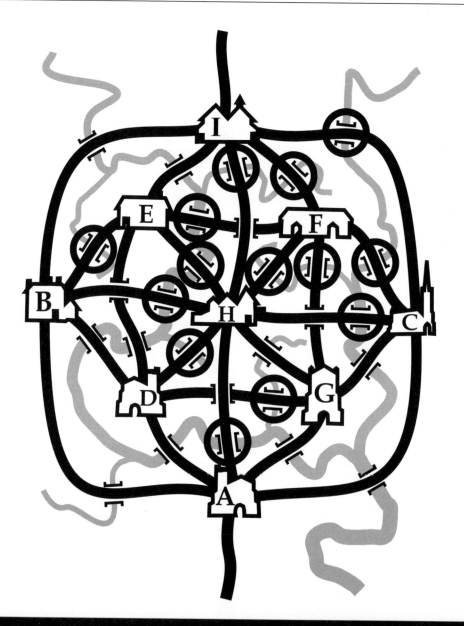

HAUNTED HOTEL

A ghost haunts one of the 45 hotel rooms listed in the chart below. A team of paranormal investigators received a list of four cryptic clues from a hotline caller reporting the sighting. Using these clues, the paranormal investigators found the room number—but by that time, the ghost had vanished. Can you find the haunted hotel room more quickly?

1. If you reversed the digits, the resulting number would be greater than 20 but less than 70.

2. The number is not divisible by 5 or 6.

3. The sum of the digits is less than 9.

4. Add 3 to the first digit to get the second digit.

51	52	53	54	55	56	57	58	59
41	42	43	44	45	46	47	48	49
31	32	33	34	35	36	37	38	39
21	22	23	24	25	26	27	28	29
11	12	13	14	15	16	17	18	19

Answer on page 175.

GRUESOME FEARS

Don't be afraid. There's no name for a fear of solving puzzles. Identify the meaning of each phobia.

1. GAMOPHOBIA

a.) Fear of gambling or games of chance

b.) Fear of hunters or hunting

c.) Fear of marriage

d.) Fear of radiation

2. GELOTOPHOBIA

a.) Fear of being laughed at

b.) Fear of cold weather

c.) Fear of ice cream or sorbet

d.) Fear of sugary foods

3. GENUPHOBIA

a.) Fear of the color green

b.) Fear of high intelligence

c.) Fear of hypocrisy

d.) Fear of knees

4. GLOBOPHOBIA

a.) Fear of balloons

b.) Fear of round objects

c.) Fear of slime

d.) Fear of travel

STEPHEN KING H_RR_R

Below is a list of Stephen King stories. The only thing is, they've lost **A, E, I, O, U,** and **Y**, as well as any punctuation and spaces between words. Can you figure out the missing vowels and decipher each title in the list below?

C R R

P T S M T R

S L M S L T

T H S H N N G

T H S T N D

JEALOUSY

Cryptograms are messages in substitution code. Break the code to read the message. For example, THE SMART CAT might become FVO QWGDF JGF if **F** is substituted for **T**, **V** for **H**, **O** for **E**, and so on.

"N DY XODRSWU SQ OZOHPLVNBF EVSUO TODWLP CSOU BSL CNO. N DY XODRSWU SQ LVO MSHLHDNL PSW VDZO MDNBLOC SQ YO. EVP UVSWRC NL AOOM EVDL N YWUL RSUO?"
—SUJDH ENRCO, LVO MNJLWHO SQ CSHNDB FHDP

WITCHES TO THE GALLOWS

In February 1692, nine-year-old Betty Parris, the daughter of a preacher brought in from Boston, began acting wildly. There was no obvious explanation for Betty's condition, but a local minister named Cotton Mather thought he had found one: Betty was a victim of witchcraft. Suspicion first fell on a Caribbean slave named Tituba, who worked in Betty's home. Tituba had been known to tell the children stories of voodoo, and was caught trying to cure Betty by feeding a "devil cake" to a dog (dogs being common forms of demons). On March 1, Tituba and two others were hauled in and examined by local magistrates. Thoroughly frightened, Tituba confessed to being a witch. Tituba's confession lit a powder keg that would claim the lives of 19 men and women before it was over. Eventually 200 townspeople were identified as witches, all of whom were thrown into jail. Governor William Phips commissioned a seven-judge court to try those accused of witchcraft. The judges found the evidence persuasive, and the court had no choice but to execute the newly discovered witches. Between June 10 and September 22, nearly 20 individuals were carted off to Gallows Hill and hanged. In May 1693, Governor Phips shut down the proceedings and freed all the remaining defendants.

BOSTON

DEVIL CAKE

DOGS

EVIL SPIRITS

EXECUTION

GALLOWS HILL

GOVERNOR PHIPS

MASSACHUSETTS

MATHER (Cotton)

PARRIS (Betty)

SALEM VILLAGE

SPECTRAL EVIDENCE

TITUBA

VOODOO

WITCHCRAFT

```
Y I J E H E U F B V M A T H E R
S J R G E Q S N T B U O H I Q I
S A O A G T T Y I O O E F P U U
P N F L A F I P T K P S K F G Z
I Q V L L A R A U V Y T T E V O
H O T I L R I R B Q Z T K O O G
P C I V O C P R A D G A Z D N T
R J U M W H S I B U C G O P B G
O Z B E S C L S F L J O A E E E
N B Z L H T I I I E V V P C L P
R N K A I I V V P R F C J P G M
E P X S L W E X E C U T I O N K
V G X N L D O G S A W X M H W C
O U O C V C U D K B W J M V X V
G V G S T T E S U H C A S S A M
S P E C T R A L E V I D E N C E
```

Answers on page 175.

SQUARE MAZE

Navigate the twisting path to find your way out of these endless corridors.

end ▲

▲
start

NORSE MONSTERS

Unscramble each word or phrase below to reveal a creature of Norse folklore.

DJ MANGO RUN

DR HULA

FIN ERR

FIR FAN

GUARD RA

JAR TON

LEG NERD

REAM

SOME FINGERS

STROLL

SAY WHAT?

Below is a group of words that, when properly arranged in the blanks, reveal a quote from *The Strange Case of Dr. Jekyll and Mr. Hyde* by Robert Louis Stevenson.

ALERT AMBITION AWAKE EVIL OCCASION

PROJECTED SLUMBERED

"At that time my virtue _____; my _____, kept _____ by _____,

was _____ and swift to seize the _____; and the thing that was

_____ was Edward Hyde."

Answers on page 176.

HAUNTED HOTEL

A ghost haunts one of the 45 hotel rooms listed in the chart below. A team of paranormal investigators received a list of four cryptic clues from a hotline caller reporting the sighting. Using these clues, the paranormal investigators found the room number—but by that time, the ghost had vanished. Can you find the haunted hotel room more quickly?

1. The number is not a multiple of 7.

2. The second digit is larger than the first digit by either one or two.

3. The number is not prime.

4. The number cannot be divided by 3 or 23.

51	52	53	54	55	56	57	58	59
41	42	43	44	45	46	47	48	49
31	32	33	34	35	36	37	38	39
21	22	23	24	25	26	27	28	29
11	12	13	14	15	16	17	18	19

COVER THAT FACE!

Cryptograms are messages in substitution code. Break the code to read the message. For example, THE SMART CAT might become FVO QWGDF JGF if **F** is substituted for **T**, **V** for **H**, **O** for **E**, and so on.

"FWXA TO YTIO OWX LEMFP CTPX FTZ
UME JXCD OM IOTAP XEXLO, OWXEX YTZ,
ATJXP TAP DQOQUBY MA OWX REMBAP,
OWX GEBQIXP TAP GEMJXA GMPZ MU T
ZMBAR CTA TGMBO OWQEOZ. WQI WTQE
TAP GEMF FXEX FWQOX—AMO REXZ
FQOW TRX, GBO FWQOX FQOW OWX
FWQOXAXII MU TYGQAQIC—TAP WQI XZXI
FXEX YQJX RTEAXOI. WQI WTAPI FXEX
LYXALWXP, WQI XZXI FQPX MDXA, TAP
WQI XSDEXIIQMA FTI MAX MU TARXE TAP
PQICTZ. 'LMKXE WQI UTLX!' ITQP T CTA.
'UME RTFP'I ITJX, LMKXE OWTO UTLX!'"
—W.R. FXYYI, OWX QAKQIQGYX CTA

DOMINION

Cryptograms are messages in substitution code. Break the code to read the quote and its author. For example, THE SMART CAT might become FVO QWGDF JGF if **F** is substituted for **T**, **V** for **H**, **O** for **E**, and so on.

"BOE EBSLOFTT BOE EFDBZ BOE UIF SFE

EFBUI IFME JMMJNJUBCMF EPNJOJPO PWFS

BMM." —FEHBS BMMBO QPF

ALFRED HITCHCOCK H_RR_R

Below is a list of Alfred Hitchcock films. The only thing is, they've lost **A**, **E**, **I**, **O**, **U**, and **Y**, as well as any punctuation and spaces between words. Can you figure out the missing vowels and decipher each title in the list below?

DLMFRMRDR

PSCH

RRWNDW

STRNGRSNTRN

THBRDS

HAUNTED HOTEL

A ghost haunts one of the 45 hotel rooms listed in the chart below. A team of paranormal investigators received a list of four cryptic clues from a hotline caller reporting the sighting. Using these clues, the paranormal investigators found the room number—but by that time, the ghost had vanished. Can you find the haunted hotel room more quickly?

1. The number is even.

2. The sum of the digits is odd.

3. The number is not divisible by 4.

4. If you divide the number in half, the resulting number is a non-prime number less than 10.

51	52	53	54	55	56	57	58	59
41	42	43	44	45	46	47	48	49
31	32	33	34	35	36	37	38	39
21	22	23	24	25	26	27	28	29
11	12	13	14	15	16	17	18	19

Answer on page 177.

SLEEP PARALYSIS DEMONS

Match each sleep paralysis demon to its country of origin.

1. Ammuttadori

2. Bakhtak

3. Batibat

4. Bou rattat

5. Dukak

6. Khyaak

7. Lietuvēns

8. Mara

9. Phi Am

10. Pisadeira

A. Brazil

B. Ethiopia

C. Iceland

D. Latvia

E. Morocco

F. Nepal

G. Pakistan

H. Philippines

I. Sardinia

J. Thailand

CIRCLE MAZE

Navigate the circular labyrinth to escape the monster.

Answer on page 177.

THE HAUNTED
DR. SAMUEL A MUDD HOUSE

Also known as St. Catharine, the Dr. Samuel A. Mudd House is named after Waldorf, Maryland's notable physician. Mudd famously treated an injured John Wilkes Booth the night he assassinated Abraham Lincoln. Many believe that Booth comes back to visit the house every night to rest, just as he did on the night of his crime. No matter how carefully museum staff make up the bed in the so-called "Booth Room", the impression of a human can often be seen in the bed by morning.

ABRAHAM LINCOLN	HISTORIC HOUSE
ASSASSIN	INJURED
BOOTH ROOM	JOHN WILKES BOOTH
CIVIL WAR	MARYLAND
DEFEAT OF THE (Confederacy)	MUSEUM
DR. SAMUEL A MUDD	NATIONAL REGISTER
DR. SAMUEL A MUDD HOUSE	SHOT THE PRESIDENT
ESCAPING JUSTICE	ST. CATHARINE
FORD'S THEATER	STRANGE INDENTATIONS
GHOSTS	WALDORF
HAUNTED	WASHINGTON, D.C.

```
V J A T G X J Y Q F R O D L A W N T S E
X X O N N F N D L U I E C I F A V N W S
I G Q H C L G G M M O O R H T O O B T U
E Q H S N I O A H U R N F I U I A E W O
H T I O X W R C N T Z A O C T Y C M A H
T Y N A S Y I I N K U N W A J I J D S D
F E P E L T S L Q I A R T L T B R I H D
O E S A D S S Q K L L N Z S I S Y R I U
T V N V A I E G R E E M U Y A V E I N M
A D Z S G Z S E E D S J A M K T I H G A
E R S V U H G E N N G B U H A J A C T L
F A U H X I D I R N I E O E A U H O O E
E G P S S M E E I P L R H O N R Q Q N U
D X E T V G U P R A E T A T T G B M D M
V L E X N Y A E M U S H E H N H D A C A
O R J A Z C O U S D J D T B T S F F L S
L M R B S V D L R U D N N T A A I U W R
O T X E A D G O F B M O I W O X C R V D
S J U H Y F F I M H R L Q V A H D T S A
H H A O X H I S T O R I C H O U S E S H
```

Answers on page 177.

MEND THE BRIDGES

A rampaging monster has barreled through the entire county, destroying all the bridges indicated by circles. Your job is to travel to each location—A through I, in any order—by restoring only 2 of the bridges.

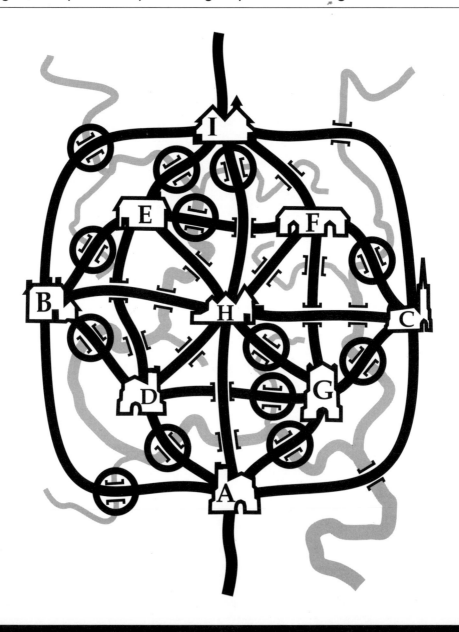

SLAVIC MONSTERS

Unscramble each word or phrase below to reveal a creature of Slavic folklore.

ASK RAUL

BAN INK

CHALK BOA

DO NAVY YO

GAR SIT

HE SLY

MAY IDLY ADD (two words)

OK AIM IRK

POET LICE

VAIL

PETER STRAUB H_RR_R

Below is a list of Peter Straub stories. The only thing is, they've lost **A, E, I, O, U,** and **Y,** as well as any punctuation and spaces between words. Can you figure out the missing vowels and decipher each title in the list below?

FYCLDSMNW

FLTNGDRGN

GHSTSTRY

JL

SHDWLND

Answers on page 178.

HORRIBLE FEARS

Don't be afraid. There's no name for a fear of solving puzzles. Identify the meaning of each phobia.

1. HALITOPHOBIA

a.) Fear of bad breath

b.) Fear of disease or illness

c.) Fear of hallways

d.) Fear of salty foods

2. HELIOPHOBIA

a.) Fear of the color red

b.) Fear of spirals

c.) Fear of the sun or sunlight

d.) Fear of vehicles

3. HEXAKOSIOIHEXEKONTA-HEXAPHOBIA

a.) Fear of closely-packed holes

b.) Fear of hexagons

c.) Fear of magicians or witches

d.) Fear of the number 666

4. HODOPHOBIA

a.) Fear of disorder or untidiness

b.) Fear of roads or streets

c.) Fear of surfing

d.) Fear of travel

Answers on page 178.

WITCHES

Match each witch to her country of origin.

1. Baba Yaga

2. Befana

3. The Bell Witch

4. Ceridwen

5. Chedipe

6. Jenny Greenteeth

7. Medea

8. Nicnevin

9. Prättäkitti

10. Yama-uba

A. England

B. Finland

C. Greece

D. India

E. Italy

F. Japan

G. Russia

H. Scotland

I. United States

J. Wales

Answers on page 178.

STEPHEN KING'S BOOKS

ACROSS

1. Programmer's language
5. Little angels
11. Big inits in movies
12. Testimony opener
14. Kazan of film
15. Clearing away
17. Govt. investigator
18. Points properly
20. Engineering detail
23. Programs in testing
26. Throw out of balance
27. Woven hat
29. Utter dully
31. RNA component
33. Eloquent one
34. Frequent beach visitor
35. Young's accounting partner
37. Physics class subject
38. Little or major follower
42. Freezer unit
44. Big bag
47. Fever with chills
48. Adaptable trucks
49. Story of a lifetime?
50. Unprevented by
51. Demonstrate delight

DOWN

1. Horror novel that tells a story of a possessed car
2. Fancy tie
3. Gym rat's pride
4. Frequent fabricator
5. Hand-held weapon
6. "Inside Man" actor Clive
7. Stephen King's book about a burial ground
8. Avenue shader
9. Crowning adornment
10. ____ Antonio Spurs
13. Brief passage
16. 2013 sequel to "The Shining"
19. Way to get a lift
21. Debit card ID
22. Musician ____ John
24. Wordlessly implied
25. Maine vampire town of fiction
28. Nourish
30. Diaz of UFC
32. Groom's last words
36. Cosmetic item
39. ____ above
40. Garden entrance, perhaps
41. Old Irish tongue
42. Unchivalrous sort
43. Motor coach
45. Kleptomaniac film monkey
46. ____ Abner

Answers on page 178.

HAUNTED HOTEL

A ghost haunts one of the 45 hotel rooms listed in the chart below. A team of paranormal investigators received a list of four cryptic clues from a hotline caller reporting the sighting. Using these clues, the paranormal investigators found the room number—but by that time, the ghost had vanished. Can you find the haunted hotel room more quickly?

1. The number either contains the digit 4 or is a multiple of 4, but not both.

2. The first digit is larger than the second digit.

3. The number is not prime.

4. The sum of the digits is even.

51	52	53	54	55	56	57	58	59
41	42	43	44	45	46	47	48	49
31	32	33	34	35	36	37	38	39
21	22	23	24	25	26	27	28	29
11	12	13	14	15	16	17	18	19

SAY WHAT?

Below is a group of words that, when properly arranged in the blanks, reveal a quote from *The Mysteries of Udolpho* by Ann Radcliffe.

ERROR ESCAPE LANGUOR PLUNGE

RELIEF VACANT WATCH

"The _____ mind is ever on the _____ for _____, and ready

to _____ into _____, to _____ from the _____ of idleness."

STEPHEN KING H_RR_R

Below is a list of Stephen King stories. The only thing is, they've lost **A, E, I, O, U**, and **Y**, as well as any punctuation and spaces between words. Can you figure out the missing vowels and decipher each title in the list below?

B G F B N S

B L C K H S

D C T R S L P

D S P R T N

M S R

PALLID MASK

Cryptograms are messages in substitution code. Break the code to read the message. For example, THE SMART CAT might become FVO QWGDF JGF if **F** is substituted for **T**, **V** for **H**, **O** for **E**, and so on.

"XSKZ KZ XSG XSKWY XSDX XPIMREGZ HG,
LIP K QDWWIX LIPYGX QDPQIZD CSGPG
REDQV ZXDPZ SDWY KW XSG SGDJGWZ;
CSGPG XSG ZSDFICZ IL HGW'Z XSIMYSXZ
EGWYXSGW KW XSG DLXGPWIIW, CSGW XSG
XCKW ZMWZ ZKWV KWXI XSG EDVG IL SDEK;
DWF HT HKWF CKEE RGDP LIP GJGP XSG
HGHIPT IL XSG NDEEKF HDZV. K NPDT YIF
CKEE QMPZG XSG CPKXGP, DZ XSG CPKXGP
SDZ QMPZGF XSG CIPEF CKXS XSKZ
RGDMXKLME, ZXMNGWFIMZ QPGDXKIW,
XGPPKREG KW KXZ ZKHNEKQKXT,
KPPGZKZXKREG KW KXZ XPMXS—D CIPEF
CSKQS WIC XPGHREGZ RGLIPG XSG VKWY KW
TGEEIC." —PIRGPX C. QSDHRGPZ, XSG VKWY
KW TGEEIC

HAUNTED HOUSES OF LITERATURE

Match each haunted house to to its original novel.

1. Allardyce House

2. Belasco House

3. Blackwood House

4. Bly House

5. Eel Marsh House

6. Manderley

7. The Navidson home

8. 112 Ocean Avenue

9. The Overlook Hotel

10. The Silver House

A. Henry James, *The Turn of the Screw* (1898)

B. Daphne du Maurier, *Rebecca* (1938)

C. Shirley Jackson, *We Have Always Lived in the Castle* (1962)

D. Richard Matheson, *Hell House* (1971)

E. Robert Marasco, *Burnt Offerings* (1973)

F. Jay Anson, *The Amityville Horror* (1977)

G. Stephen King, *The Shining* (1977)

H. Susan Hill, *The Woman in Black* (1983)

I. Mark Z. Danielewski, *House of Leaves* (2000)

J. Helen Oyeyemi, *White Is for Witching* (2009)

Answers on page 179.

SCARY HALLOWEEN

ACROSS

1. Large shark parts
5. Anchor cable hole
11. Pumpkin grinner
12. Writer Nevada ____
13. Avian chatterbox
14. Make public
16. Relating to clan
19. Small spots
21. Large-intestine bacteria
22. Show to a seat, briefly
25. Electrolysis atoms
27. Libretto portion
28. Sweet snacks on sticks
31. Old nursery rhyme king
32. Threshold of a door
33. Rehab concern, familiarly
35. Moth-eaten, e.g.
37. Gaze
39. Footless
41. Bill from an ATM
44. Near the hip
46. Times gone by
47. Halloween staple
48. Diaphanous
49. Naughty look, maybe

DOWN

2. Amsterdam football club
3. ____ speed
4. Young codfish
5. Members of one's peer group
6. One of the Khans
7. Wish
8. Backbeat component, often
9. Fair
10. England, to Caesar
12. Steady date
15. Declared
17. Not at all excited
18. Party favorites?
20. Garden creeper
23. Reporter's hope
24. Hunting cry (var.)
26. Full of irregular stains
29. Short of
30. Snowbank maker
31. Hip-shaking dance
34. Island or terrier
36. 1945 treaty city
38. Light a fire under
40. In-of link
42. Slight winning margin
43. Dendrologist's interest
45. Carpenter's tool

Answers on page 179.

MEND THE BRIDGES

A rampaging monster has barreled through the entire county, destroying all the bridges indicated by circles. Your job is to travel to each location—A through I, in any order—by restoring only 2 of the bridges.

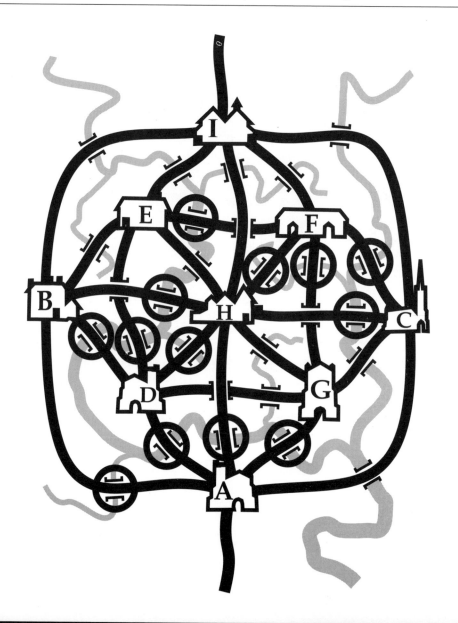

Answer on page 179.

MONSTROUS FEARS

Don't be afraid. There's no name for a fear of solving puzzles. Identify the meaning of each phobia.

1. MAGEIROCOPHOBIA

a.) Fear of cooking

b.) Fear of government

c.) Fear of lava or magma

d.) fear of magicians or witches

2. MASKLOPHOBIA

a.) Fear of dreams

b.) Fear of household appliances

c.) Fear of masseurs or massages

d.) Fear of people in costumed clothing

3. MUSOPHOBIA

a.) Fear of disorder or untidiness

b.) Fear of growing muscular

c.) Fear of mice or rats

d.) Fear of music

4. MYSOPHOBIA

a.) Fear of contamination, dirt, or germs

b.) Fear of fungus and mold

c.) Fear of heavy machinery

d.) Fear of the unknown

Answers on page 180.

DAVID CRONENBERG H_RR_R

Below is a list of David Cronenberg films. The only thing is, they've lost **A, E, I, O, U,** and **Y**, as well as any punctuation and spaces between words. Can you figure out the missing vowels and decipher each title in the list below?

DDRNGRS

THBRD

THDDZN

THFL

VDDRM

MASK

Cryptograms are messages in substitution code. Break the code to read the message. For example, THE SMART CAT might become FVO QWGDF JGF if **F** is substituted for **T**, **V** for **H**, **O** for **E**, and so on.

"HEA KBYZ MG YAUG-TASAWHFMV LBY VM

UMVNAX B KBYZ GMX KA, FH LBY B WBXH

MG KA." —XMDAXH L. SEBKDAXY, HEA ZFVN

FV RAUUML

SQUARE MAZE

Navigate the twisting path to find your way out of these endless corridors.

start

end

Answer on page 180.

MYTHICAL CREATURES

BASILISK	MANTICORE
BIGFOOT	MERMAID
CENTAUR	MINOTAUR
CHIMERA	NESSIE
CYCLOPS	OGRE
DRAGON	PEGASUS
FAIRY	PHOENIX
GNOME	PIXIE
GRIFFIN	SPHINX
KAPPA	TROLL
KELPIE	UNICORN
LEPRECHAUN	YETI

```
M R F C B U A S D T A P P A K P
N X T D S Z R C E R S C S L L E
E I P L E K E E T J A K D D G G
P G H R D Q M N R R M G V O D A
I R T R L C I T J I O S O S I S
X I L O L E H A Z E X L P N A U
I F V E O O C U G R B O L W M S
E F D N P G B R V O L Z E L R O
J I Y C Y R D Z D C C K R T E A
I N N U W E E I Y I Y P K J M D
Z V S J C A T C D T E I S S E N
D H G N O M E I H N O W A A D K
L S P H I N X P B A S I L I S K
I U R U A T O N I M U M G O V P
H Y R I A F A P H O E N I X X E
E U N I C O R N E B I G F O O T
```

GREEK MONSTERS

Unscramble each word or phrase below to reveal a creature of Greek folklore.

BIRCH DAYS

CREMATION

CURB SEER

HARDY

HI CREAM

HOP MUSIC APP

MAIN TOUR

NOG ORG

PYTHON

RINSE

SAY WHAT?

Below is a group of words that, when properly arranged in the blanks, reveal a quote from *Dracula* by Bram Stoker.

BRING FREELY HAPPINESS HOUSE

LEAVE SAFELY WELCOME

"_____ to my _____. Come _____. Go _____; and _____

something of the _____ you _____!"

SUPERSTITION

Cryptograms are messages in substitution code. Break the code to read the message. For example, THE SMART CAT might become FVO QWGDF JGF if **F** is substituted for **T**, **V** for **H**, **O** for **E**, and so on.

"DVL MRFLCMDZDZEI RFEI XVZOV DVZM DKNL ZM YERIULU ZM JLCT QLILCKN ZI DVL LKMD. KBEIQ DVL KCKGZKIM ZD KFFLKCM DE GL OEBBEI: ZD UZU IED, VEXLJLC, LADLIU ZDMLNY DE DVL QCLLWM RIDZN KYDLC DVL LMDKGNZMVBLID EY OVCZMDZKIZDT; KIU ZD VKM EINT KMMRBLU ZDM FCLMLID YECB MZIOL DVL UZJJZMZEI EY DVL NKDZI KIU QCLLW OVRCOVLM; KD XVZOV DZBL, DVL ZULK GLOEBZIQ FCLJKNLID, DVKD K NKDZI GEUT OERNU IED OECCRFD ZY GRCZLU ZI DVLZC DLCCZDECT, ZD QCKURKNNT ZIOCLKMLU, KIU YECBLU DVL MRGHLOD EY BKIT XEIULCYRN MDECZLM, MDZNN LADKID, EY DVL ULKU CZMZIQ YCEB DVLZC QCKJLM, KIU YLLUZIQ RFEI DVL GNEEU EY DVL TERIQ KIU GLKRDZYRN." —HEVI XZNNZKB FENZUECZ, DVL JKBFTCL

HAUNTED HOTEL

A ghost haunts one of the 45 hotel rooms listed in the chart below. A team of paranormal investigators received a list of four cryptic clues from a hotline caller reporting the sighting. Using these clues, the paranormal investigators found the room number—but by that time, the ghost had vanished. Can you find the haunted hotel room more quickly?

1. The number is larger than 3 cubed but smaller than 7 squared.

2. The number is prime.

3. The second digit is larger than the first.

3. When the digits are multiplied together, the resulting number is odd.

51	52	53	54	55	56	57	58	59
41	42	43	44	45	46	47	48	49
31	32	33	34	35	36	37	38	39
21	22	23	24	25	26	27	28	29
11	12	13	14	15	16	17	18	19

HAUNTED HOTEL PROVINCIAL (PART I)

(Read this haunted account, then turn to the next page to test your knowledge.)

The Hotel Provincial is one of the most haunted locations in New Orleans. This inn, which is located in the city's famed French Quarter, is made up of five different buildings. Even though they can't order room service, many of the Hotel Provincial's ghosts have decided to extend their stays…eternally.

Thought to be the most haunted part of the hotel, the "500 building" dates back to 1722 and was used as a hospital during the War of 1812's Battle of New Orleans (December 1814–January 8, 1815) and during the Civil War. Specters of soldiers from both wars have been seen roaming the halls and imploring guests for help. In one room, guests have glimpsed soldiers moaning in pain, but when the lights are turned on, the room is empty. Bloodstains have appeared—and disappeared—on hotel bedding. And one employee who was riding the elevator was taken by surprise when the doors opened to reveal a hospital ward full of medical staff tending to wounded soldiers. Stunned, the employee remained on the elevator so long that the doors closed; when they opened again, the wartime scene had vanished.

One hotel guest reported being pulled from her bed by an invisible force, and a young girl said that she emerged from a shower to find a pile of bloody bandages on the floor; they quickly disappeared. On the lighter side, a ghost who seems enamored with country music inhabits one room, while another resident spirit likes a specific rock-and-roll radio station; when guests try to change the channel, the tuner mysteriously returns to the one that the unseen visitor prefers.

Throughout the hotel, observers have experienced doors that open and close on their own, whispering when no one else is around, hot spots, cold spots, and phantom figures wandering the property. An older woman even woke up one night to find the upper half of a handsome young soldier in her bed; one can only imagine how she explained that to her husband!

HAUNTED HOTEL PROVINCIAL (PART II)

(Do not read this until you have read the previous page!)

1. The Hotel Provincial is made up of three different buildings.

_____ True

_____ False

2. Before it was a hotel, what did the function of the "500 building" used to be?

A. Hospital

B. Library

C. Post office

D. Prison

3. A young girl emerged from a shower to find a pile of broken glass on the floor.

_____ True

_____ False

4. The older woman woke up to find which part of a soldier's body in her bed:

A. Right arm

B. Right leg

C. Torso

D. Upper half

VAMPIRES OF LITERATURE

Match these famous vampires of literature to their original stories.

1. Akasha

2. Clarimonde

3. Edward Cullen

4. Joshua York

5. Kurt Barlow

6. Lestat de Lioncourt

7. Lord Ruthven

8. Matthew Clairmont

9. Mircalla

10. Shori

A. John William Polidori, "The Vampire" (1819)

B. Théophile Gautier, "La Morte Amoureuse" (1836)

C. Joseph Sheridan Le Fanu, *Carmilla* (1872)

D. Stephen King, *'Salem's Lot* (1975)

E. Anne Rice, *Interview with the Vampire* (1976)

F. George R.R. Martin, *Fevre Dream* (1982)

G. Anne Rice, *The Queen of the Damned* (1988)

H. Octavia E. Butler, *Fledgling* (2005)

I. Stephanie Meyer, *Twilight* (2005)

J. Deborah Harkness, *A Discovery of Witches* (2011)

Answers on page 181.

THE HAUNTED ST. ELMO GHOST TOWN

St. Elmo, Colorado, was founded in 1880 as a mining town. For four decades, nearly 2,000 people called the town home, but in the early 1920s, the mining industry declined, and the population dwindled. Today, a handful of people still live in St. Elmo, but for the most part, the ghost town is an empty shell of its former self. And no ghost town would be complete without a ghost or two; St. Elmo's most famous spirit is Annabelle Stark, a former resident who is now often seen gazing from the upstairs window of a hotel.

ANNABELLE STARK

CHAFFEY COUNTY

CLOSED DOWN

COLORADO

DENVER, SOUTH PARK,
(and Pacific Railroad)

GHOST TOWN

GOLD PROSPECTORS

HISTORIC DISTRICT

LOW POPULATION

MARY MURPHY MINE
(Most Successful in the Area)

MINING TOWN

SALOON

SAWATCH RANGE

SILVER PROSPECTORS

ST. ELMO

TOWN HALL

TOWN JAIL

UPSTAIRS WINDOW

```
S B E B Z L Y V W L Q N S U Q W A K G X
P R K L B J N Z J X W N P E B B R J I N
U L O Y S G L Q B O R S M I S A O H G D
N L A T V T O C D X T P G L T C I O M L
N H L V C P E D C A H I M S I L L X S D
R S J A I E E L I D Z I E M O D T Y A E
S V V C H S P R M J N L C W P E C T W N
H D D V O N S S N O L S P R B O F N A V
P C A L O W W I O E M O O N Z D C U T E
M G C O I R G O B R P S W R T A Q O C R
B H L N S O R A T U P O D O C R Q C H S
P A D D Y T N E L E T R W X B O H Y R O
S O G P N N W A C T J N E H E L D E A U
W C R A A D T T S P J U Q V L O Y F N T
L A P R H I O O B A R X S J L C G F G H
Y O N E O R H J I U Y A F F U I A A E P
Z T Z N S G X L M K Y T L R Y H S H U A
T C I R T S I D C I R O T S I H Z C B R
Y N E N I M Y H P R U M Y R A M A X M K
B O X T U P F G D N W O T G N I N I M E
```

Answers on page 181.

CROSSOVER MAZE

Cross over and under tunnels to reach the end of the underground lair.

▼start

end ▼

MEND THE BRIDGES

A rampaging monster has barreled through the entire county, destroying all the bridges indicated by circles. Your job is to travel to each location—A through I, in any order—by restoring only 2 of the bridges.

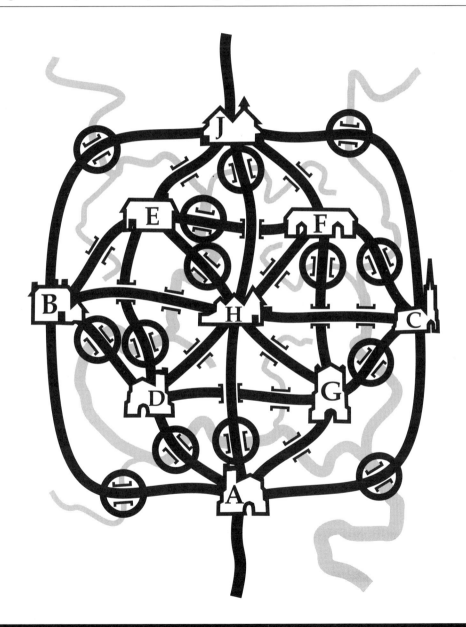

Answer on page 182.

WEST AFRICAN MONSTERS

Unscramble each word or phrase below to reveal a creature of West African folklore.

A BIO

A GOAT MONK

A NANKIN INK (two words)

ABS MOAN

BEAN JOG

DAZE

HAIR

I OAF BOY

MEEK BLOB MEME

OAKEN AMULET

ANNE RICE H_RR_R

Below is a list of Anne Rice stories. The only thing is, they've lost **A, E, I, O, U,** and **Y,** as well as any punctuation and spaces between words. Can you figure out the missing vowels and decipher each title in the list below?

L S H R

N T R V W W T H T H V M P R

T H Q N F T H D M N D

T H V M P R L S T T

T H W T C H N G H R

NIGHTMARISH FEARS

Don't be afraid. There's no name for a fear of solving puzzles. Identify the meaning of each phobia.

1. NOCTIPHOBIA

   a.) Fear of clouds

   b.) Fear of the moon

   c.) Fear of night

   d.) Fear of sleepwalking

2. NOMOPHOBIA

   a.) Fear of being out of mobile phone contact

   b.) Fear of the color orange

   c.) Fear of the government or ruling powers

   d.) Fear of graphs or charts

3. NOSOPHOBIA

   a.) Fear of congestion or mucus

   b.) Fear of contracting a disease

   c.) Fear of doctors or medical tests

   d.) Fear of noses

4. NOSOCOMEPHOBIA

   a.) Fear of being alone

   b.) Fear of death

   c.) Fear of fatigue

   d.) Fear of hospitals

Answers on page 182.

HAUNTED PLACES

Match each haunted location to its American state.

1. Begich Towers

2. The Crescent Hotel and Spa

3. Fort Morgan

4. Hotel Monte Vista

5. Lums Pond State Park

6. Norwich State Hospital

7. Oakland Cemetery

8. St. Augustine Lighthouse

9. Stanley Hotel

10. Winchester Mystery House

A. Mobile Point, Alabama

B. Whittier, Alaska

C. Flagstaff, Arizona

D. Eureka Springs, Arkansas

E. San Jose, California

F. Estes Park, Colorado

G. Preston, Connecticut

H. Bear, Delaware

I. St. Augustine, Florida

J. Atlanta, Georgia

HAUNTED HOTEL

A ghost haunts one of the 45 hotel rooms listed in the chart below. A team of paranormal investigators received a list of four cryptic clues from a hotline caller reporting the sighting. Using these clues, the paranormal investigators found the room number—but by that time, the ghost had vanished. Can you find the haunted hotel room more quickly?

1. The number is odd.

2. The sum of its digits is even.

3. The number is not prime.

4. The sum of its digits is a cube number.

51	52	53	54	55	56	57	58	59
41	42	43	44	45	46	47	48	49
31	32	33	34	35	36	37	38	39
21	22	23	24	25	26	27	28	29
11	12	13	14	15	16	17	18	19

Answer on page 183.

SCARY MONSTERS

ACROSS

1. Cathedral city in north France
8. Scratch
12. Verdant
13. Web access enabler: abbr.
14. Fine-tune
15. ____ von Bismarck
16. "All Things Considered" network
17. Tiny screen symbol
18. Largest of the Marianas
19. ____ Scala, actress
20. Confab
21. Imaginary monster
24. Terrier's bark
27. Hard wood pin
28. Get rid of
31. Sorrowful through deprivation
33. Rubbishy
34. Steeple
35. Put to the test
36. NYSE unit
37. Grotesquely carved figure
40. Scrooge utterances
42. Stiff bristle
43. Impudence
47. Low female choir voices
48. Fannie ____
49. Threesome
50. "Tres ____!"
51. Miss after marriage
52. Nobleman
53. Warbled
54. Accumulated on the surface

DOWN

1. Wooden soles footwear
2. Tutsi mortal enemies
3. Dog star
4. Diamond shape
5. Malaysian money
6. Spotted
7. Waterfall effect
8. Bustling Great Lakes port
9. Scottish lake with legendary serpent
10. Indonesian ox
11. Left
22. Proposal
23. ____ Streep, actress
24. Washboard ____
25. Weightlifting unit
26. Cause fear in
29. Cryptographic network protocol: abbr.
30. Norse war god
32. Removing from existence
33. Abstinence
35. In the direction of
38. Dangerous rays
39. Organic compound
40. Streisand, in headlines
41. Inter ____
44. Oman native
45. King's title
46. Convinced

Answers on page 183.

SAY WHAT?

Below is a group of words that, when properly arranged in the blanks, reveal a quote from *The Legend of Sleepy Hollow* by Washington Irving.

COMMON COQUETTE ENTITLED HERO RENOWN

UNDISPUTED WINS

"He who _____ a thousand _____ hearts, is therefore _____ to some _____; but he who keeps _____ sway over the heart of a _____, is indeed a _____."

GUILLERMO DEL TORO H_RR_R

Below is a list of Guillermo del Toro films. The only thing is, they've lost **A, E, I, O, U,** and **Y,** as well as any punctuation and spaces between words. Can you figure out the missing vowels and decipher each title in the list below?

CRMSNPK

CRNS

MMC

PNSLBRNTH

THDVLSBCKBN

MONSTROUS LAWS

Cryptograms are messages in substitution code. Break the code to read the message. For example, THE SMART CAT might become FVO QWGDF JGF if **F** is substituted for **T**, **V** for **H**, **O** for **E**, and so on.

"CX IUX QOTFNKXS LBU BOU UXLONIAN.

XWXUR FVQOANX ZKIZ CX NZUFWX ZB

NZUITPAX GUBBSN FT ZKX VFTS ITS

QBFNBTN ON. ZKX GBSR NFTN BTEX, ITS KIN

SBTX CFZK FZN NFT, LBU IEZFBT FN I VBSX

BL QOUFLFEIZFBT. TBZKFTP UXVIFTN ZKXT

GOZ ZKX UXEBAAXEZFBT BL I QAXINOUX, BU

ZKX AOMOUR BL I UXPUXZ. ZKX BTAR CIR ZB

PXZ UFS BL I ZXVQZIZFBT FN ZB RFXAS ZB

FZ. UXNFNZ FZ, ITS RBOU NBOA PUBCN

NFED CFZK ABTPFTP LBU ZKX ZKFTPN FZ KIN

LBUGFSSXT ZB FZNXAL, CFZK SXNFUX LBU

CKIZ FZN VBTNZUBON AICN KIWX VISX

VBTNZUBON ITS OTAICLOA." —BNEIU CFASX,

ZKX QFEZOUX BL SBUFIT PUIR

MORE HAUNTED PLACES

Match each haunted location to its American state.

1. The Bates Motel

2. Dr. Samuel A. Mudd House

3. Eldridge Hotel

4. Hull House

5. Independence State Hospital

6. 'Iolani Palace

7. Liberty Hall

8. Museums of Old York

9. The Myrtles Plantation

10. Nicholson-Rand House

A. Honolulu, Hawai'i

B. Coeur d'Alene, Idaho

C. Chicago, Illinois

D. Indianapolis, Indiana

E. Independence, Iowa

F. Lawrence, Kansas

G. Frankfort, Kentucky

H. St. Francisville, Louisiana

I. York, Maine

J. Waldorf, Maryland

SQUARE MAZE

Navigate the twisting path to find your way out of these endless corridors.

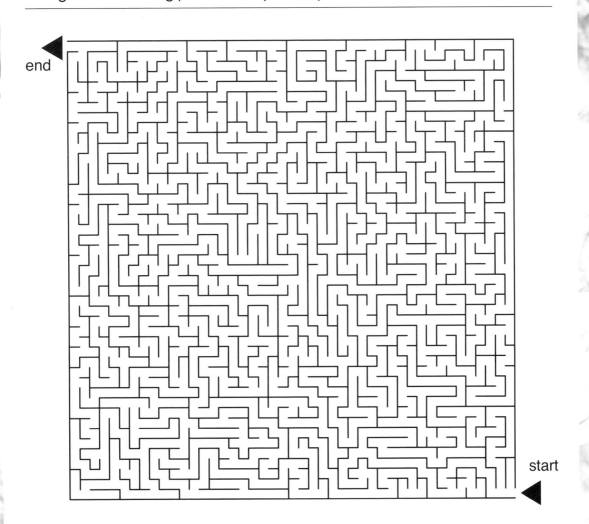

end

start

Answer on page 184.

MEND THE BRIDGES

A rampaging monster has barreled through the entire county, destroying all the bridges indicated by circles. Your job is to travel to each location—A through I, in any order—by restoring only 2 of the bridges.

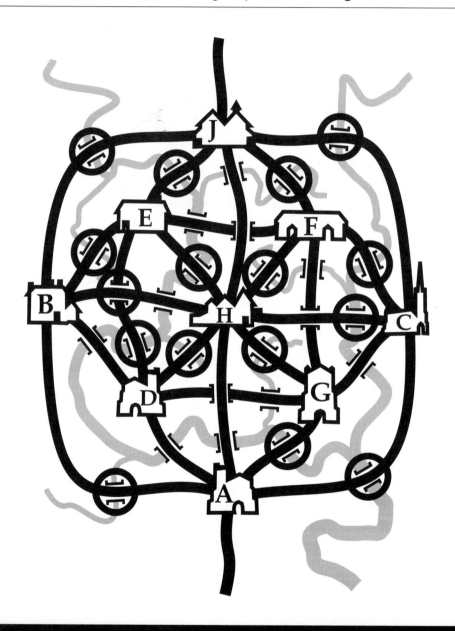

HAUNTED HOTEL

A ghost haunts one of the 45 hotel rooms listed in the chart below. A team of paranormal investigators received a list of four cryptic clues from a hotline caller reporting the sighting. Using these clues, the paranormal investigators found the room number—but by that time, the ghost had vanished. Can you find the haunted hotel room more quickly?

1. The sum of the digits is greater than 5.

2. When the digits are multiplied, the resulting number is less than 25.

3. The number is prime.

4. Add 6 to the smaller digit to get the larger digit.

51	52	53	54	55	56	57	58	59
41	42	43	44	45	46	47	48	49
31	32	33	34	35	36	37	38	39
21	22	23	24	25	26	27	28	29
11	12	13	14	15	16	17	18	19

Answer on page 184.

OUTRAGEOUS FEARS

Don't be afraid. There's no name for a fear of solving puzzles. Identify the meaning of each phobia.

1. OIKOPHOBIA

a.) Fear of fats or oils

b.) Fear of garlic or onions

c.) Fear of household appliances

d.) Fear of imperfections

2. OMMETAPHOBIA

a.) Fear of cheese

b.) Fear of eyes

c.) Fear of loud noises

d.) Fear of meditation

3. ONEIROPHOBIA

a.) Fear of birds

b.) Fear of dreams

c.) Fear of obligations

d.) Fear of sleeping in public places

4. OSMOPHOBIA

a.) Fear of odors

b.) Fear of salt

c.) Fear of stars and space

d.) Fear of tastes

SHADOWY BOUNDARIES

Cryptograms are messages in substitution code. Break the code to read the quote and its author. For example, THE SMART CAT might become FVO QWGDF JGF if **F** is substituted for **T**, **V** for **H**, **O** for **E**, and so on.

"RFC ZMSLBYPGCQ UFGAF BGTGBC JGDC

DPMK BCYRF YPC YR ZCQR QFYBMUW YLB

TYESC. UFM QFYJJ QYW UFCPC RFC MLC

CLBQ, YLB UFCPC RFC MRFCP ZCEGLQ?"

—CBEYP YJJYL NMC

H_RR_R G_NR_S

Below is a list of horror genres. The only thing is, they've lost **A, E, I, O, U,** and **Y,** as well as any punctuation and spaces between words. Can you figure out the missing vowels and decipher each genre in the list below?

S P R N T R L

S R V V L

V M P R

W T C H C R F T

Z M B

EDGAR ALLAN POE

AMONTILLADO

"ANNABEL LEE"

ARTHUR GORDON PYM

"THE BALLOON-HOAX"

CRYPTOGRAPHY

DETECTIVE FICTION

DUPIN

"EUREKA"

GOTHIC

HOUSE OF USHER

"LENORE"

MACABRE

MASQUE

NEVERMORE

PIT

POETRY

PENDULUM

PURLOINED

RED DEATH

"THE RAVEN"

ROMANTICISM

"TAMERLANE"

"THE TELL-TALE HEART"

"TO HELEN"

VIRGINIA CLEMM

WRITER

```
R H P I D H T A E D D E R X T A G G M
E S O I A O F R K W E L T I H O A L K
T Y E W I X I B D K T W P R T G W U X
I E T H E T E L L T A L E H E A R T T
R U R I S A V I R G I N I A C L E M M
W R Y J W Z F E R B A C A M O Y L A X
E E L L E B A N N A X M A Y D M E T J
E K O J F H X Y K S C N U U L Q N H C
N A N E L E H O T I M M V L U X O E W
A R O M A N T I C I S M I C U X R R O
L X A O H N O O L L A B E H T D E A K
R V G P U R L O I N E D Y K N P N V P
E Q P N O I T C I F E V I T C E T E D
M Q P O F M P E H D T S J F T S Q N P
A U O W A U Y H O U S E O F U S H E R
T T Y S L U C R Y P T O G R A P H Y B
S A Q R A R J H T I N E V E R M O R E
A U U K Y Q A M O N T I L L A D O E R
E A R T H U R G O R D O N P Y M Y S I
```

Answers on page 185.

SQUARE MAZE

Navigate the twisting path to find your way out of these endless corridors.

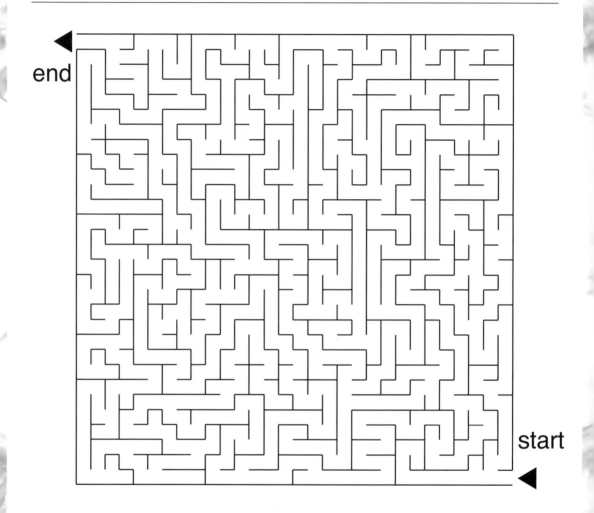

end

start

SAY WHAT?

Below is a group of words that, when properly arranged in the blanks, reveal a quote from Bela Lugosi.

DON'T MIGHT NEVER PERSONALLY VAMPIRE

"I have _____ met a _____ _____, but I _____ know

what _____ happen tomorrow."

INDIAN MONSTERS

Unscramble each word or phrase below to reveal a creature of Indian folklore.

A BOOTH

AHA CHIPS

ANY HAVANA BOA THROAT (three words)

ASK SARAH

CHEAPEN PINCH

HIYA SINK

HUM VIA KITE

IN HIS

MT HAIKU IRK

TAPER

Answers on page 185.

A FIGURE ON HORSEBACK

Cryptograms are messages in substitution code. Break the code to read the message. For example, THE SMART CAT might become FVO QWGDF JGF if **F** is substituted for **T**, **V** for **H**, **O** for **E**, and so on.

"QWZ SHNEOROQ UGEIEQ, WHTZBZI, QWRQ WRAOQU QWEU ZOPWROQZS IZCEHO, ROS UZZNU QH FZ PHNNROSZI-EO-PWEZJ HJ RDD QWZ GHTZIU HJ QWZ REI, EU QWZ RGGRIEQEHO HJ R JECAIZ HO WHIUZFRPV, TEQWHAQ R WZRS. EQ EU URES FM UHNZ QH FZ QWZ CWHUQ HJ R WZUUERO QIHHGZI, TWHUZ WZRS WRS FZZO PRIIEZS RTRM FM R PROOHO-FRDD, EO UHNZ ORNZDZUU FRQQDZ SAIEOC QWZ IZBHDAQEHORIM TRI, ROS TWH EU ZBZI ROS ROHO UZZO FM QWZ PHAOQIM JHDV WAIIMEOC RDHOC EO QWZ CDHHN HJ OECWQ, RU EJ HO QWZ TEOCU HJ QWZ TEOS." —TRUWEOCQHO EIBEOC, QWZ DZCZOS HJ UDZZGM WHDDHT

YALE'S SPIRITED ORGANIST (PART 1)

(Read this haunted account, then turn to the next page to test your knowledge.)

You know that an institution is rich with history when it is old enough to have celebrated its 300th anniversary in 2001. That's the case with Yale University, which opened its doors in New Haven, Connecticut, in 1701. While ghosts of students, professors, and even early colonists surely remain on these storied grounds, one particular area of Yale has quite a reputation for being haunted: Woolsey Hall.

Built in 1901—in recognition of the university's 200th anniversary—Woolsey Hall is the institution's main auditorium. It seats more than 2,500 people and has hosted performances by several symphonies, as well as rock concerts; but its ghosts aren't quite so fond of the latter.

The haunting of the building centers on the 1902 construction of the Newberry Memorial Organ—one of the largest and most renowned organs in the world. It is named for the Newberry family, which made a large donation to fund the instrument's upkeep. Harry B. Jepson, the school's first organist, played and maintained the pipe organ, but it periodically became outdated. The Newberry family stepped up to fund improvements to the organ in 1915 and 1928 to keep it state-of-the-art.

But in the 1940s, Yale forced Jepson to retire, and he never again played the Newberry Organ. While unhappy with this turn of events, the organist seemingly made peace with his situation—at least until the hall began hosting rock concerts. Some say that the last straw was when Jimi Hendrix played at Woolsey Hall on November 17, 1968. When Jepson's ghost saw this beautiful concert hall used for rock-and-roll music, he became angry.

Since that time, workers and visitors have reported feeling a menacing presence and a sense of evil in the hall, especially near the organ chambers and in the basement. People have heard the organ playing when the auditorium is locked and no one is sitting at the bench. One thing is certain: Jepson won't be playing any rock-and-roll music.

YALE'S SPIRITED ORGANIST (PART II)

(Do not read this until you have read the previous page!)

1. What year did Yale University open its doors?

A. 1701

B. 1705

C. 1710

D. 1711

2. Approximately how many people can Woolsey Hall seat?

A. 2,250

B. 2,500

C. 2,750

D. 3,000

3. What is the name of the school's first organist?

A. Barry B. Benson

B. Harry B. Jepson

C. Harvey B. Johnson

D. Jerry B. Henson

4. Jimi Hendrix's performance at Woolsey Hall was the ghostly organist's final straw.

____ True

____ False

HAUNTED HOTEL

A ghost haunts one of the 45 hotel rooms listed in the chart below. A team of paranormal investigators received a list of four cryptic clues from a hotline caller reporting the sighting. Using these clues, the paranormal investigators found the room number—but by that time, the ghost had vanished. Can you find the haunted hotel room more quickly?

1. The number is even.

2. The sum of its digits is even.

3. The number can't be divided by 11.

4. The sum of its digits is greater than 10.

51	52	53	54	55	56	57	58	59
41	42	43	44	45	46	47	48	49
31	32	33	34	35	36	37	38	39
21	22	23	24	25	26	27	28	29
11	12	13	14	15	16	17	18	19

Answer on page 186.

HORROR MOVIE ICONS

Match each actor to the horror movie icon they portrayed.

1. Bolaji Badejo

A. Count Orlok, *Nosferatu* (1922)

2. Doug Bradley

B. Count Dracula, *Dracula* (1931)

3. Ricou Browning

C. The Monster, *Frankenstein* (1931)

4. Nick Castle

D. Gill-man, *Creature from the Black Lagoon* (1954)

5. Robert Englund

E. Godzilla, *Godzilla* (1954)

6. Gunnar Hansen

F. Leatherface, *The Texas Chain Saw Massacre* (1974)

7. Boris Karloff

8. Bela Lugosi

G. Michael Myers, *Halloween* (1978)

9. Haruo Nakajima

H. Xenomorph, *Alien* (1979)

10. Max Schreck

I. Freddy Krueger, *Nightmare on Elm Street* (1984)

J. Pinhead, *Hellraiser* (1987)

JOHN CARPENTER H_RR_R

Below is a list of John Carpenter films. The only thing is, they've lost **A, E, I, O, U,** and **Y,** as well as any punctuation and spaces between words. Can you figure out the missing vowels and decipher each title in the list below?

H L L W N

N T H M T H F M D N S S

P R N C F D R K N S S

T H F G

T H T H N G

ALONE

Cryptograms are messages in substitution code. Break the code to read the message. For example, THE SMART CAT might become FVO QWGDF JGF if **F** is substituted for **T, V** for **H, O** for **E,** and so on.

"WS XUXSAG CSYL UJXFUZ JG ZUGAQMWL,
JKL UL LCQAQMWL WS CFKAZ MF FKL
PKNNASZ KB QYRQDQJAG, CWSLWSX LWS
CSULWSX CSXS EFAZ FX YFL, UYZ WS EWFDS
LWS AFYSAQSDL BULWD UYZ LWFDS PFDL
FRSXDWUZFCSZ JG LXSSD UYZ JUYID."
—W.M. CSAAD, LWS QYRQDQJAS PUY

THE HAUNTED GARNET GHOST TOWN

The Garnet Ghost Town in Drummond, Montana, is considered the state's best preserved ghost town. Dating back to 1895, the town was named for the ruby-colored, semi-precious stones found in the mines nearby, yet gold was the main draw for the prospectors who came to the town. But only ten years later, the mining began to dwindle; Garnet was a ghost town by the 1940s. Today, it draws ghost hunters, who say Kelly's Saloon is the most haunted building in town. The sounds of music, laughter, and slamming doors are often heard in the empty building.

ABANDONED	HAUNTED TOWN
APPARITIONS	KELLY'S SALOON
DRUMMOND	MINERS
EMPTY BUILDINGS	PHANTOM LAUGHTER
GARNET GHOST TOWN	PHANTOM MUSIC
GHOST HUNTERS	PROSPECTORS
GHOSTS	SLAMMING DOORS
GOLD MINE	WELL PRESERVED

```
A P P A R I T I O N S P X X H Y F N D N
Q U G E Z T M I N E R S G G R W X N R O
Y S R O O D G N I M M A L S H T O E G U
D S C M O T V V U J A H S A Z M T Z R Y
E G D O Y G M A B G C R U Q M H X R O L
N H Z E V G E M Q F O Q F U G C M N V E
O O D D V K A G D T A I R U G C S N L U
D S V G B R H R C G A D A J H R G K V F
N T D Y D O E E N F M L U A B P N N L N
A H Y Z S Z P S I E M M U E H P I D O U
B U Z T E S G X E O T N S A X Q D O B L
A N S L O B D O R T G N A Y D L Y G A
N T A R H J D N L E P T H A U A I M S I
Z E P P K S A L D D O L Y O S E U K A D
V R D K Q H W T A M M F L S S Q B D C W
E S Z D P T O T M N N I Y E R T Y G N Y
Z X O N O W R U J S K L N C W Q T M K J
R Y A C N Z S F U P L Q Q E Y F P O N L
S R R K A I C E D E Y W A I J J M O W G
V T E Q C G E O K S M G N R V U E V Z N
```

MEND THE BRIDGES

A rampaging monster has barreled through the entire county, destroying all the bridges indicated by circles. Your job is to travel to each location—A through I, in any order—by restoring only 2 of the bridges.

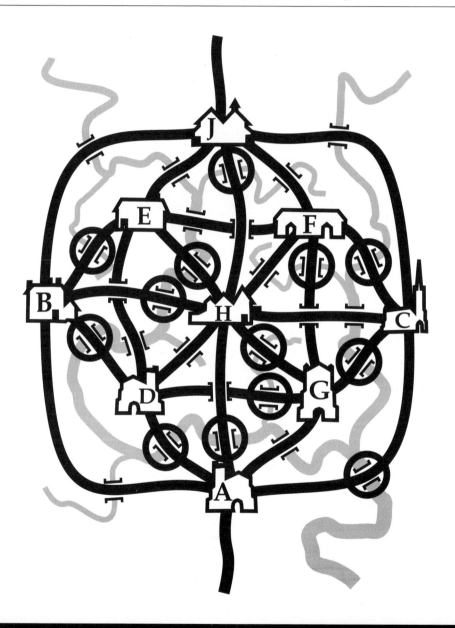

JAPANESE MONSTERS

Unscramble each word or phrase below to reveal a creature of Japanese folklore.

A BIKE RUN

A NEON URN

AHA MICA KIT

BOA IRONY

HUG OAK ROADS

ION

MIMIC YOU HOUR

MOO OR JUG

SKIM AUTO GUM

SUN KITE

SAM RAIMI H_RR_R

Below is a list of Sam Raimi films. The only thing is, they've lost **A**, **E**, **I**, **O**, **U**, and **Y**, as well as any punctuation and spaces between words. Can you figure out the missing vowels and decipher each title in the list below?

DRGMTHLL

DRKMN

RMFDRKNSS

THGFT

THVLDD

PETRIFYING FEARS

Don't be afraid. There's no name for a fear of solving puzzles. Identify the meaning of each phobia.

1. PHAGOPHOBIA

a.) Fear of congestion or mucus

b.) Fear of disease or illness

c.) Fear of swallowing

d.) Fear of yawning

2. PHILOPHOBIA

a.) Fear of being scared

b.) Fear of love

c.) Fear of philosophy

d.) Fear of social gatherings

3. POGONOPHOBIA

a.) Fear of beards

b.) Fear of dancing

c.) Fear of lizards

d.) Fear of poison

4. PORPHYROPHOBIA

a.) Fear of the color purple

b.) Fear of rocks or boulders

c.) Fear of volcanoes

d.) Fear of whales or porpoises

MORE HORROR MOVIE ICONS

Match each actor to the horror movie icon they portrayed.

1. Bonnie Aarons

2. Joseph Bishara

3. Javier Botet

4. Daveigh Chase

5. Matthew Patrick Davis

6. Kevin Peter Hall

7. Doug Jones

8. Tim Purcell

9. Bill Skarsgård

10. David Howard Thornton

A. Predator, *The Predator* (1987)

B. Samara Morgan, *The Ring* (2002)

C. The Pale Man, *Pan's Labyrinth* (2006)

D. Lipstick-Face Demon, *Insidious* (2010)

E. The Babadook, *The Babadook* (2014)

F. Valek, *The Conjuring 2* (2016)

G. Art the Clown, *Terrifier* (2016)

H. Pennywise, *It* (2017)

I. Slender Man, *Slender Man* (2018)

J. The Mother, *Barbarian* (2022)

THINGS THAT GO BUMP IN THE NIGHT

ACROSS

1. Owl yowl
5. Vincent Price or Peter Lorre, e.g.
10. Surg. specialty
11. Ali's boxing daughter
12. Some horror film creatures
14. Irish lullaby syllable
15. "____ fan tutte" (Mozart opera)
16. Widow in "Peer Gynt"
18. Chaney of horror films
19. 1982 Adrienne Barbeau movie
23. Wheels, to adolescents
24. Brazil's ____ Paulo
25. Calcutta's continent
27. Removable car roofs
31. Scary campfire narrative
33. Bursts of wind
34. ____ Bator (Mongolia's capital)
35. Haunted-house figure
36. Halloween fliers

DOWN

1. Bay at the moon
2. Best-selling cookie
3. Other, in Acapulco
4. Zodiac's Aries
5. Greeting on el telefono
6. Advanced math class, for short
7. Copenhagen's ____ Gardens
8. "Little House" antagonist Nellie ____
9. Demolition work, in Devon
13. Fliers with narrow waists
17. States, in France
19. "Lido Shuffle" singer Boz
20. Get clean before dinner
21. Like an opera song
22. Jacuzzi product
26. Regarding, in a memo
28. "Star Wars" green-skinned dancer
29. It comes before a fall
30. Thesaurus entries, briefly
32. Cluck of disapproval

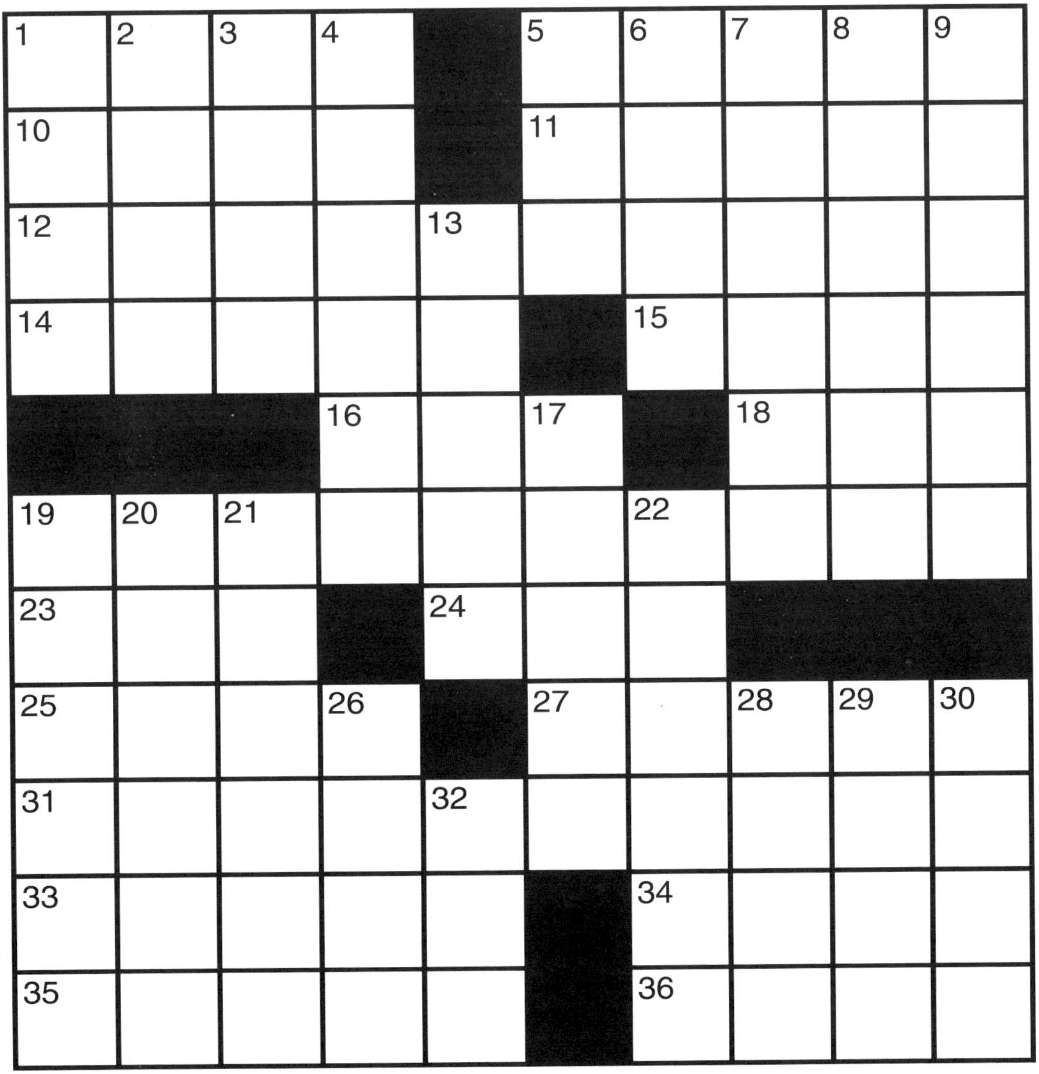

Answers on page 187.

HAUNTED HOTEL

A ghost haunts one of the 45 hotel rooms listed in the chart below. A team of paranormal investigators received a list of four cryptic clues from a hotline caller reporting the sighting. Using these clues, the paranormal investigators found the room number—but by that time, the ghost had vanished. Can you find the haunted hotel room more quickly?

1. The number is odd.

2. The number is not prime.

3. When the digits are multiplied together, the resulting number is odd.

4. The sum of the digits is divisible by 8.

51	52	53	54	55	56	57	58	59
41	42	43	44	45	46	47	48	49
31	32	33	34	35	36	37	38	39
21	22	23	24	25	26	27	28	29
11	12	13	14	15	16	17	18	19

SAY WHAT?

Below is a group of words that, when properly arranged in the blanks, reveal a quote from *The Picture of Dorian Gray* by Oscar Wilde.

ALWAYS   COMMIT   COURAGE   FOND

NEVER   REPRESENT   SINS

"Yes, Dorian, you will _____ be _____ of me. I _____ to you all

the _____ you _____ had the _____ to _____."

DARIO ARGENTO H_RR_R

Below is a list of Dario Argento films. The only thing is, they've lost **A, E, I, O, U**, and **Y**, as well as any punctuation and spaces between words. Can you figure out the missing vowels and decipher each title in the list below?

D P R D

N F R N

P H N M N

S S P R

T H M T H R F T R S

Answers on pages 187 & 188.

UNEQUAL BARGAIN

Cryptograms are messages in substitution code. Break the code to read the message. For example, THE SMART CAT might become FVO QWGDF JGF if **F** is substituted for **T**, **V** for **H**, **O** for **E**, and so on.

"ID HMZI SC VO EDI LSIN UYWOEE, LMZ ID QSY ID INDZY MRRYISIYZ LNSHN S NMQ EDCJ ZYHAYIEO SCQTEJYQ MCQ NMQ DG EMIY XYJTC ID RMVRYA. ID HMZI SI SC LSIN NOQY, LMZ ID QSY ID M INDTZMCQ SCIYAYZIZ MCQ MZRSAMISDCZ, MCQ ID XYHDVY, MI M XEDL MCQ GDAYBYA, QYZRSZYQ MCQ GASYCQEYZZ. INY XMAJMSC VSJNI MRRYMA TCYFTME; XTI INYAY LMZ ZISEE MCDINYA HDCZSQYAMISDC SC INY ZHMEYZ; GDA LNSEY UYWOEE LDTEQ ZTGGYA ZVMAISCJEO SC INY GSAYZ DG MXZISCYCHY, NOQY LDTEQ XY CDI YBYC HDCZHSDTZ DG MEE INMI NY NMQ EDZI." —ADXYAI EDTSZ ZIYBYCZDC, INY ZIAMCJY HMZY DG QA. UYWOEE MCQ VA. NOQY

VAMPIRIC MONSTERS

Match each vampiric monster to its country of origin.

---

1. Abhartach

2. Asema

3. Jiangshi

4. Mandurugo

5. Penanggalan

6. Ramanga

7. Sasabonsam

8. Soucouyant

9. Strigoi

10. Strzyga

A. China

B. Ghana

C. Ireland

D. Madagascar

E. Malaysia

F. Philippines

G. Poland

H. Romania

I. Suriname

J. Trinidad

Answers on page 188.

CIRCLE MAZE

Navigate the circular labyrinth to escape the monster.

MEND THE BRIDGES

A rampaging monster has barreled through the entire county, destroying all the bridges indicated by circles. Your job is to travel to each location—A through I, in any order—by restoring only 2 of the bridges.

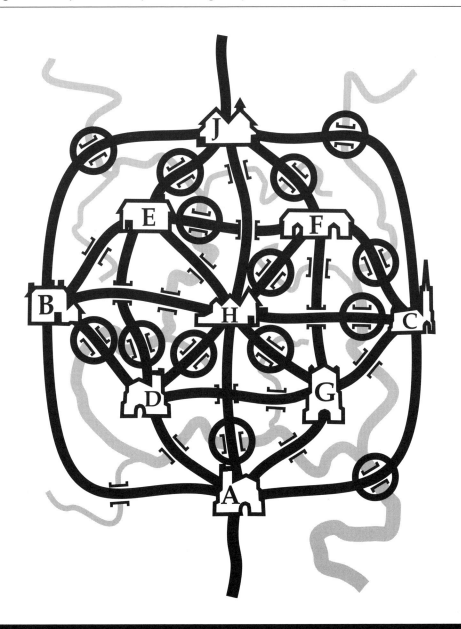

Answer on page 188.

SPINE-CHILLING FEARS

Don't be afraid. There's no name for a fear of solving puzzles. Identify the meaning of each phobia.

1. SCOPOPHOBIA

a.) Fear of being stared at

b.) Fear of doctors or medical tests

c.) Fear of school

d.) Fear of scorpions

2. SIDERODROMOPHOBIA

a.) Fear of heavy metals

b.) Fear of running

c.) Fear of stars and space

d.) Fear of trains

3. SPHEKSOPHOBIA

a.) Fear of the color yellow

b.) Fear of round objects

c.) Fear of travel

d.) Fear of wasps

4. SUBMECHANOPHOBIA

a.) Fear of caves or caverns

b.) Fear of deep water

c.) Fear of heavy machinery

d.) Fear of submerged man-made objects

MIKE FLANAGAN H_RR_R

Below is a list of Mike Flanagan TV shows. The only thing is, they've lost **A**, **E**, **I**, **O**, **U**, and **Y**, as well as any punctuation and spaces between words. Can you figure out the missing vowels and decipher each title in the list below?

MDNGHTMSS

THFLLFTHHSFSHR

THHNTNGFBLMNR

THHNTNGFHLLHS

THMDNGHTCLB

SEA OF WONDERS

Cryptograms are messages in substitution code. Break the code to read the message. For example, THE SMART CAT might become FVO QWGDF JGF if **F** is substituted for **T**, **V** for **H**, **O** for **E**, and so on.

"E WA WSS EC W GHW VY DVCIHTG. E IVPFN; E YHWT; E NXECU GNTWCRH NXECRG, DXEQX E IWTH CVN QVCYHGG NV AJ VDC GVPS. RVI UHHL AH, EY VCSJ YVT NXH GWUH VY NXVGH IHWT NV AH!" —FTWA GNVUHT, ITWQPSW

Answers on page 188 & 189.

DRACULA

ARTHUR

BRAM

CARPATHIA

DRACULA

ENGLAND

GARLIC

HARKER

JONATHAN

LUCY

MINA

QUINCEY

RENFIELD

ROMANIA

SEWARD

SLEEPWALKING

STOKER

TRANSYLVANIA

VAMPIRE

VAN HELSING

WESTERNA

R T V K F G Q F W N T P K S S C
O J R A O F A P M J V M T T E L
M O N A I Q W R V I A G O W R M
A N D V N H W M L R N K X V G A
N A R M Y S T E B I E A L L N R
I T A O C Q Y A K R C U Y X I T
A H W H U D U L P B K E Q D S H
V A E G L O A I V R B C T N L U
D N S P A W Z V N A A M U A E R
G E R I P M A V J C N C E L H N
T E O E L Z V Q U N E I J G N L
Q A E G I P W H A T D Y A N A K
I L I K X Y V P L O M C J E V X
S Z M L D I A N R E T S E W W S
Y O M P N Q C V L D R A C U L A
V R E N F I E L D H A R K E R U

Answers on page 189.

SQUARE MAZE

Navigate the twisting path to find your way out of these endless corridors.

end

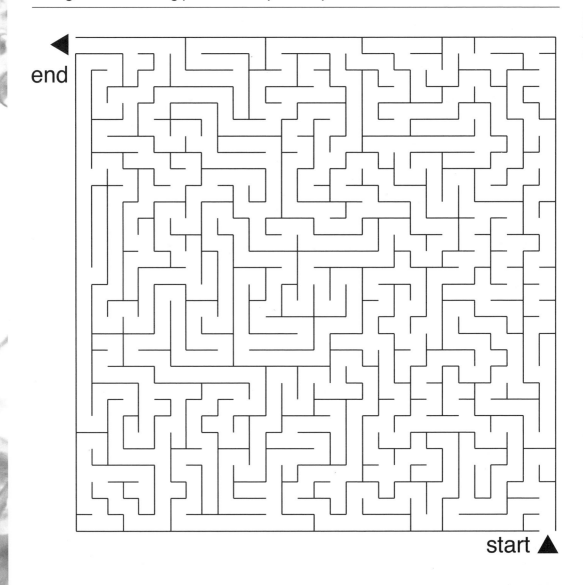

start

INDONESIAN MONSTERS

Unscramble each word or phrase below to reveal a creature of Indonesian folklore.

ABATIS NAP

ANGEL NAP NAG

BARGAIN NOUN
(two words)

BEEPING BAT
(two words)

COP NOG

DNA RAG

LEAKY

ONLY BORING
(two words)

OOH LA

TO BIJOU
(two words)

UNAKIN TALK

SAY WHAT?

Below is a group of words that, when properly arranged in the blanks, reveal a quote from *The Strange Case of Dr. Jekyll and Mr. Hyde* by Robert Louis Stevenson.

BALANCE   CAPACIOUS   CONDESCENSION   DESTROYED

END   FILLED   SOUL

"There comes an _____ to all things; the most _____ measure

is _____ at last; and this brief _____ to evil finally _____

the _____ of my _____."

CLEVER MAN

Cryptograms are messages in substitution code. Break the code to read the message. For example, THE SMART CAT might become FVO QWGDF JGF if **F** is substituted for **T**, **V** for **H**, **O** for **E**, and so on.

"ZQL YHF TCFWFH BYI, JHMFIG KQPI; ZQL HFYNQI EFCC, YIG ZQLH EMS MN OQCG; OLS ZQL YHF SQQ DHFKLGMTFG. ZQL GQ IQS CFS ZQLH FZFN NFF IQH ZQLH FYHN PFYH, YIG SPYS EPMTP MN QLSNMGF ZQLH GYMCZ CMJF MN IQS QJ YTTQLIS SQ ZQL. GQ ZQL IQS SPMIV SPYS SPFHF YHF SPMIAN EPMTP ZQL TYIIQS LIGFHNSYIG, YIG ZFS EPMTP YHF; SPYS NQBF DFQDCF NFF SPMIAN SPYS QSPFHN TYIIQS? OLS SPFHF YHF SPMIAN QCG YIG IFE EPMTP BLNS IQS OF TQISFBDCYSF OZ BFI'N FZFN, OFTYLNF SPFZ VIQE—QH SPMIV SPFZ VIQE—NQBF SPMIAN EPMTP QSPFH BFI PYWF SQCG SPFB." —OHYB NSQVFH, GHYTLCY

CROSSOVER MAZE

Cross over and under tunnels to reach the end of the underground lair.

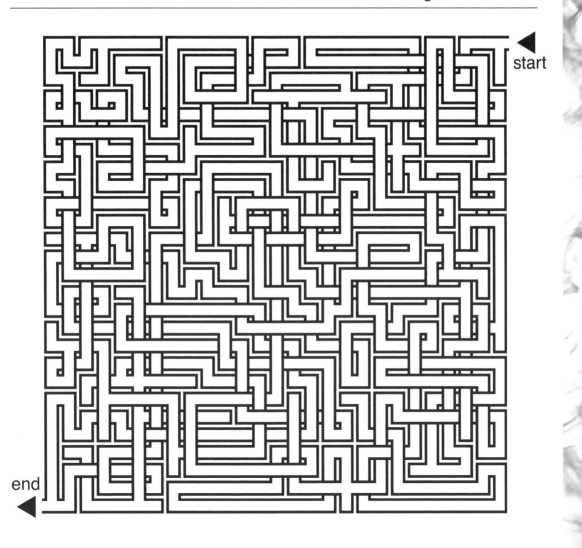

start

end

Answer on page 190.

WES CRAVEN H_RR_R

Below is a list of Wes Craven films. The only thing is, they've lost **A**, **E**, **I**, **O**, **U**, and **Y**, as well as any punctuation and spaces between words. Can you figure out the missing vowels and decipher each title in the list below?

N G H T M R N L M S T R T

N W N G H T M R

S C R M

T H H L L S H V S

T H P P L N D R T H S T R S

CRUEL LOVE

Cryptograms are messages in substitution code. Break the code to read the message. For example, THE SMART CAT might become FVO QWGDF JGF if **F** is substituted for **T**, **V** for **H**, **O** for **E**, and so on.

"LXC DKUU GQKOA TS MNCSU, PSNL HSUBKHQ, ECG UXPS KH JUDJLH HSUBKHQ; GQS TXNS JNVSOG GQS TXNS HSUBKHQ." —ZXHSRQ HQSNKVJO US BJOC, MJNTKUUJ

HAUNTED HOTEL

A ghost haunts one of the 45 hotel rooms listed in the chart below. A team of paranormal investigators received a list of four cryptic clues from a hotline caller reporting the sighting. Using these clues, the paranormal investigators found the room number—but by that time, the ghost had vanished. Can you find the haunted hotel room more quickly?

---

1. The number is a multiple of either 3 or 4, but not both.

2. The sum of the digits is not a prime number.

3. If you reverse the digits, the resulting number is greater than 50.

4. The sum of the digits is less than 9.

51	52	53	54	55	56	57	58	59
41	42	43	44	45	46	47	48	49
31	32	33	34	35	36	37	38	39
21	22	23	24	25	26	27	28	29
11	12	13	14	15	16	17	18	19

Answer on page 190.

HORROR GAMES

Match each playable character to their horror video game.

1. Amanda Ripley

2. Chris Redfield

3. Daniel

4. Harry Mason

5. Joel Miller

6. Leon S. Kennedy

7. Miku Hinasaki

8. Miles Upshur

9. Point Man

10. The Stranger

A. *Resident Evil* (1996)

B. *Resident Evil 2* (1998)

C. *Silent Hill* (1999)

D. *Fatal Frame* (2001)

E. *F.E.A.R.* (2005)

F. *Amnesia: The Dark Descent* (2010)

G. *The Last of Us* (2013)

H. *Outlast* (2013)

I. *Alien: Isolation* (2014)

J. *Darkwood* (2014)

PETER STRAUB H_RR_R

Below is a list of Peter Straub stories. The only thing is, they've lost **A**, **E**, **I**, **O**, **U**, and **Y**, as well as any punctuation and spaces between words. Can you figure out the missing vowels and decipher each title in the list below?

D R K M T T R

K K

L S T B L S T G R L

N T H N G H T R M

T H T L S M N

THIS LITTLE VALLEY

Cryptograms are messages in substitution code. Break the code to read the message. For example, THE SMART CAT might become FVO QWGDF JGF if **F** is substituted for **T**, **V** for **H**, **O** for **E**, and so on.

"FG SMSO F ZUXWIQ HFZU GXO L OSJOSLJ
HUFJUSO F BFVUJ ZJSLI GOXB JUS HXOIQ
LTQ FJZ QFZJOLKJFXTZ, LTQ QOSLB NWFSJIA
LHLA JUS OSBTLTJ XG L JOXWEISQ IFGS, F
DTXH XG TXTS BXOS YOXBFZFTV JULT JUFZ
IFJJIS MLIISA." —JUS ISVSTQ XG ZISSYA
UXIIXH

HAUNTINGS IN CONNECTICUT

BARA-HACK

BENTON HOMESTEAD

DEVIL'S HOPYARD

DOWNS ROAD

EVERGREEN CEMETERY

FAIRFIELD HILLS

GLEBE HOUSE

GREEN MANOR

HOOKMAN'S CEMETERY

HUBBARD PARK

LEDGE LIGHTHOUSE

LITCHFIELD INN

OLD NEWGATE PRISON

PETTIBONE TAVERN

POLI-PALACE THEATER

RED BROOK INN

SAVOY HOTEL

SEASIDE

SHUBERT THEATER

UNION CEMETERY

WARNER THEATER

YANKEE PEDLAR INN

```
H R U F A I R F I E L D H I L L S B F U
N N E N S A V O Y H O T E L C N S A I C
U E C T Q K Q Y X P S Y L P O Y O C E P
H Q S U A K R B K S A I A S T P O V V O
O O C U N E E A E C T W I B E Y E N R L
H R O B O G H A P C A R X T Z R U N E I
R Y J K H H S T H D P H T Q G L D I T P
L J R L M I T F T E R I A R L L D R A A
O D R E D A I H T R B A E R R Z E A E L
G I O E T E N A G O E E B E A G V L H A
X L M W L E G S N I N B D B R B I D T C
G R E D N W M E C C L B U E U H L E R E
L K I B E S T E E R E E H I H S P E T
Q N J N E A R M C O M N G W S P H E N H
N P D H V H E O O N M E C D S L O E R E
G L U E Z T O K A A O Y T Q E V P K A A
O Y R F E F I U N D S I V E E L Y N W T
Z N A R M N D O S R E H N V R T A A E E
Z W Y F N E R U F E U L F U E Y R Y I R
I G B E N T O N H O M E S T E A D N A N
```

Answers on page 191.

MEND THE BRIDGES

A rampaging monster has barreled through the entire county, destroying all the bridges indicated by circles. Your job is to travel to each location—A through I, in any order—by restoring only 2 of the bridges.

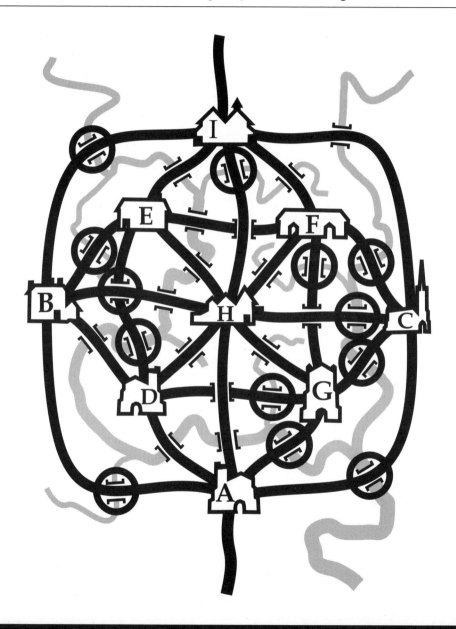

AUSTRALIAN MONSTERS

Unscramble each word or phrase below to reveal a creature of Australian folklore.

AHOY AWAY HARM

ASPEN HOOK
(two words)

BORED RAP
(two words)

BRAINPOWER NEST
(two words)

BUY PIN

DID I TALK

JUG MEND WALK

JUROR BURN

PUNISHABLE TOURNAMENT
(three words)

UNWORTHY BEAVER SMIRKERS
(three words)

JAMES WAN H_RR_R

Below is a list of James Wan films. The only thing is, they've lost **A, E, I, O, U,** and **Y,** as well as any punctuation and spaces between words. Can you figure out the missing vowels and decipher each title in the list below?

DDSLNC

MLGNNT

NSDS

SW

THCNJRNG

Answers on page 191.

TERRIFYING FEARS

Don't be afraid. There's no name for a fear of solving puzzles. Identify the meaning of each phobia.

1. THALASSOPHOBIA

a.) Fear of actors

b.) Fear of deep water

c.) Fear of rhetorical questions

d.) Fear of whips

2. TOKOPHOBIA

a.) Fear of childbirth or pregnancy

b.) Fear of the color blue

c.) Fear of feet or toes

d.) Fear of memories or memory loss

3. TRISKAIDEKAPHOBIA

a.) Fear of crossing streets

b.) Fear of the number 13

c.) Fear of public speaking

d.) Fear of sugary foods

4. TRYPOPHOBIA

a.) Fear of dentists

b.) Fear of holes

c.) Fear of insects

d.) Fear of marriage

Answers on page 191.

MORE HORROR GAMES

Match each playable character to their horror video game.

1. Alex

2. The Hunter

3. Isaac Clarke

4. Laura Kearney

5. Mike Munroe

6. Mike Schmidt

7. Rebecca Owens

8. Sebastian Castellanos

9. Simon Jarrett

10. Six

A. *The Evil Within* (2014)

B. *Five Nights at Freddy's* (2014)

C. *Bloodborne* (2015)

D. *SOMA* (2015)

E. *Until Dawn* (2015)

F. *Oxenfree* (2016)

G. *Little Nightmares* (2017)

H. *The Mortuary Assistant* (2022)

I. *The Quarry* (2022)

J. *Dead Space* (2023)

Answers on page 191.

DRACULA

ACROSS

1. Stephen King specialty
10. Ginger Spice Halliwell
11. Cornhusker's st.
12. Rubbish rummager
13. Hot spiced wines
16. Nat or Natalie
18. Pretentious and showy
20. "Turandot" slave girl
22. Gleaming
24. Dominica surrounder: abbr.
25. Grand Central, e.g.
26. Falco of "The Sopranos"
29. One of the 50-Across's abilities
33. Prefix with chute or graph
34. Nicknamed
35. Azure expanse
36. 1950s Egyptian VIP
38. Type of culture
39. Toyland denizens
41. Newsom or Belinsky
43. Anterior wings in beetles
46. Attempt to find out
48. Garner, as rewards
49. Former boxing champ Max
50. Famous blooddrinker

DOWN

1. Neighbor of Fr.
2. Delphic
3. Milosevic's predecessor
4. Takes in
5. Disney film frame
6. Cable staple
7. Donor's offering
8. Reddish-brown color
9. Stringy and viscous
14. Hail
15. Hand grip
17. Zap with a beam
19. Wasted
21. Ivy League town
23. Laughs
27. Dumping
28. "The Mummy" setting
30. Commission
31. Japanese art
32. Casino game
37. Still
39. Election Day group
40. Gallant
42. Sir, to a Hindu
44. Small child
45. Dog's warning
47. Large parrot

Answers on page 191.

HAUNTED HOTEL

A ghost haunts one of the 45 hotel rooms listed in the chart below. A team of paranormal investigators received a list of four cryptic clues from a hotline caller reporting the sighting. Using these clues, the paranormal investigators found the room number—but by that time, the ghost had vanished. Can you find the haunted hotel room more quickly?

---

1. The number is either a square or cube number.

2. The sum of its digits is less than 10.

3. The sum of its digits is greater than 7.

4. If you subtract 20 from the number, the resulting number is a square number

51	52	53	54	55	56	57	58	59
41	42	43	44	45	46	47	48	49
31	32	33	34	35	36	37	38	39
21	22	23	24	25	26	27	28	29
11	12	13	14	15	16	17	18	19

SAY WHAT?

Below is a group of words that, when properly arranged in the blanks, reveal a quote from *Frankenstein* by Mary Shelley.

ALONE ASSOCIATES DESOLATION ENEMY FALLEN

FRIENDS MALIGNANT

"The _____ angel becomes a _____ devil. Yet even that _____ of

God and man had _____ and _____ in his _____; I am _____."

M. NIGHT SHYAMALAN H_RR_R

Below is a list of M. Night Shyamalan films. The only thing is, they've lost **A, E, I, O, U,** and **Y,** as well as any punctuation and spaces between words. Can you figure out the missing vowels and decipher each title in the list below?

K N C K T T H C B N

S G N S

S P L T

T H S X T H S N S

T H V L L G

Answers on page 192.

TRANSPARENT

Cryptograms are messages in substitution code. Break the code to read the message. For example, THE SMART CAT might become FVO QWGDF JGF if **F** is substituted for **T**, **V** for **H**, **O** for **E**, and so on.

"ZQF GXZ AWVV WOIVXLG. L BWGWGRWB
PMXP DLYMP. LP AXN VXPW XP DLYMP—LD
PMW HXZPLGW QDW AXN RQPMWBWH ALPM
PMW YXCLDY, NLVVZ NPFHWDPN—XDH L
AQBUWH PMWD NQGWPLGWN PLVV HXAD. LP
IXGW NFHHWDVZ, NCVWDHLH XDH
IQGCVWPW LD GZ GLDH. L AXN XVQDW;
PMW VXRQBXPQBZ AXN NPLVV, ALPM PMW
PXVV VLYMPN RFBDLDY RBLYMPVZ XDH
NLVWDPVZ. LD XVV GZ YBWXP GQGWDPN L
MXSW RWWD XVQDW. 'QDW IQFVH GXUW XD
XDLGXV—X PLNNFW—PBXDNCXBWDP! QDW
IQFVH GXUW LP LDSLNLRVW! XVV WOIWCP
PMW CLYGWDP—L IQFVH RW LDSLNLRVW!'
L NXLH, NFHHWDVZ BWXVLNLDY AMXP LP
GWXDP PQ RW XD XVRLDQ ALPM NFIM
UDQAVWHYW. LP AXN QSWBAMWVGLDY."
—M.Y. AWVVN, PMW LDSLNLRVW GXD

TOP TEN HORROR FILMS

Place these top ten highest-grossing horror films as of January 2024 in order.

1.

2.

3.

4.

5.

6.

7.

8.

9.

10.

A. *The Exorcist* (1973)

B. *The Sixth Sense* (1999)

C. *Hannibal* (2001)

D. *Signs* (2002)

E. *I Am Legend* (2007)

F. *Prometheus* (2012)

G. *World War Z* (2013)

H. *It* (2017)

I. *The Nun* (2018)

J. *It Chapter Two* (2019)

Answers on page 192.

THE HAUNTED WINCHESTER MYSTERY HOUSE

At first glance, the Winchester Mystery House looks like a typical Queen-Anne Victorian-style home. But inside the 24,000-square-foot mansion is a mysterious interior that many claim is haunted. Some of the doors and stairs to the 161-room home lead to nowhere, and spider web motifs and the No. 13 are used in various ways throughout the house. One thing is certain: this mysterious mansion is not to be messed with.

ABANDONED

ARCHITECTURAL

CALIFORNIA

CONSTRUCTION

CURIOSITIES

DOORS TO NOWHERE

FIREARM MAGNATE

HAUNTED

LABYRINTH

MANSION

QUEEN ANNE VICTORIAN

REPEATING RIFLES

SAN JOSE

SARAH WINCHESTER

SHADOWY FIGURES

TOURIST ATTRACTION

WILLIAM WIRT (Winchester)

WINCHESTER MYSTERY (House)

WINCHESTER REPEATING (Arms Co.)

WINCHESTER RIFLE

WINDING HALLWAYS

```
W S N O I T C A R T T A T S I R U O T E
I Y C O N S T R U C T I O N T I H A M W
N A I R O T C I V E N N A N E E U Q I I
C W N E S O J N A S U P S A S G L Z N N
H L C G F J N F Q J H E B A E I A S D C
E L H G Z F I D Q T I A R R R R K E H H
S A A H Z D K N N T N A W C U E Q L M E
T H U G J S R I I D H I N H G Y Z F S S
E G N R D B R S O W L Z O I I O I I J T
R N T Y M Y O N I L E O I T F O J R Z E
R I E T B I E N I O U B S E Y W X G A R
I D D A R D C A E Y Q Z N C W U R N I R
F N L U H H M V S I W O A T O E L I N E
L I C E E W Q P B W Q J M U D W L T R P
E W D S I J J M J W C M E R A V R A O E
N M T R J V B V S R W F K A H D V E F A
E E T P B B C E B P Q R O L S V B P I T
R A T F I R E A R M M A G N A T E E L I
W I N C H E S T E R M Y S T E R Y R A N
R Q E R E H W O N O T S R O O D C S C G
```

Answers on page 192.

SQUARE MAZE

Navigate the twisting path to find your way out of these endless corridors.

start ▼

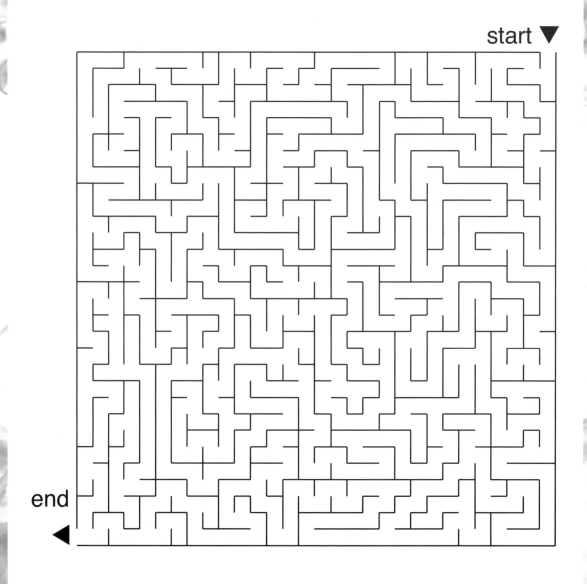

end

◄

MEND THE BRIDGES

A rampaging monster has barreled through the entire county, destroying all the bridges indicated by circles. Your job is to travel to each location—A through I, in any order—by restoring only 2 of the bridges.

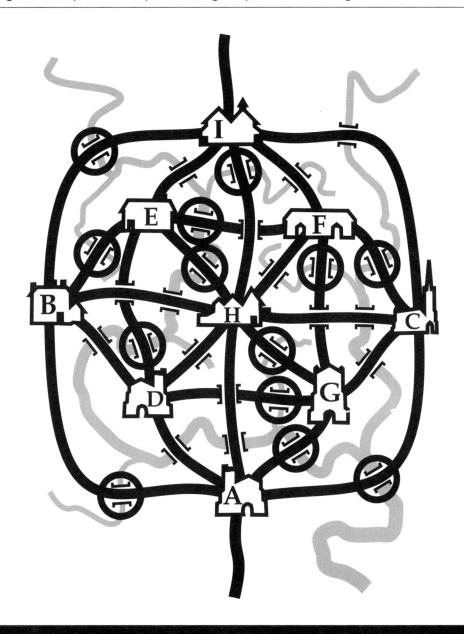

Answer on page 192.

AWFUL FEARS (page 4)

1. A; 2. D; 3. C; 4. A

LIFE AMONG THE SANE (page 5)

"I became insane, with long intervals of horrible sanity."
—Edgar Allan Poe

POE ST_R__S (page 5)

"Berenice"; "Ligeia"; "The Fall of the House of Usher"; "The Man of the Crowd"; "William Wilson"

GHOST STORY (page 6)

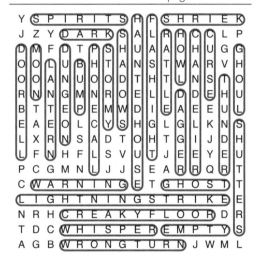

SQUARE MAZE (page 8)

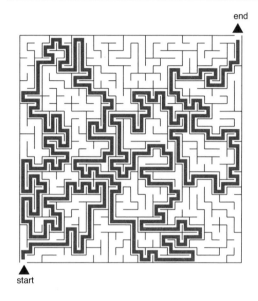

SAY WHAT? (page 9)

"Sleep, those little slices of death, how I loathe them."

NORTH AMERICAN CRYPTIDS (page 9)

Chupacabra; Hodag; Fresno Nightcrawler; Flathead Lake Monster; Beast of Busco; Jackalope; Dover Demon; Jersey Devil; Bigfoot; Flatwoods Monster

DEATH'S HOUSE (page 10)

"Yes, death. Death must be so beautiful. To lie in the soft brown earth, with the grasses waving above one's head, and listen to silence. To have no yesterday, and no to-morrow. To forget time, to forget life, to be at peace. You can help me. You can open for me the portals of death's house, for love is always with you, and love is stronger than death is."
—Oscar Wilde, "The Canterville Ghost"

FOND DU LAC GHOSTS (PART II) (page 12)

1. C; 2. A; 3. B; 4. D

HAUNTED HOTEL (page 13)

The answer is 56.

BEST-SELLING HORROR NOVELS (page 14)

1. D. *Frankenstein* (1818); 2. A. *Dracula* (1897); 3. E. *The Haunting of Hill House* (1959); 4. B. *The Exorcist* (1971); 5. I. *The Shining* (1977); 6. C. *Flowers in the Attic* (1979); 7. G. *Pet Sematary* (1983); 8. F. *It* (1986); 9. J. *The Silence of the Lambs* (1988); 10. H. *Ring* (1991)

CIRCLE MAZE (page 15)

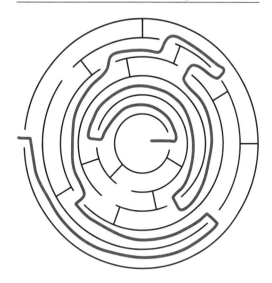

ANSWER KEY

THE HAUNTED ALCATRAZ ISLAND (page 16)

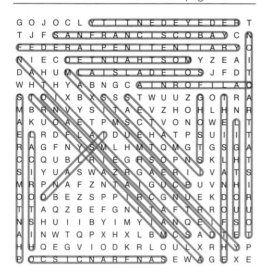

MEND THE BRIDGES (page 18)

Answers may vary.

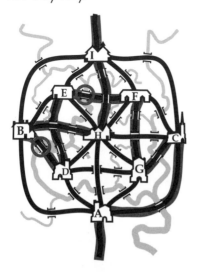

MORE NORTH AMERICAN CRYPTIDS (page 19)

Sasquatch; Pope Lick Monster; Tennessee Wildman; Snallygaster; Shunka Warakin; Skunk Ape; Wampus Cat; Mothman; Loveland Frogman; Pukwudgie

H_RR_R G_NR_S (page 19)

Body; Comedic; Crime; Demonic Possession; Apocalyptic

BONE-CHILLING FEARS (page 20)

1. C; 2. A; 3. D; 4. A

MORBID MUSE (page 21)

"The death then of a beautiful woman is unquestionably the most poetical topic in the world, and equally is it beyond doubt that the lips best suited for such topic are those of a bereaved lover."
—Edgar Allan Poe

POE P__MS (page 21)

"A Dream Within A Dream"; "Lenore"; "Annabel Lee"; "The Bells"; "The Raven"

GHOSTS OF LITERATURE (page 22)

1. F; 2. B; 3. C; 4. D; 5. G; 6. A; 7. E; 8. J; 9. H; 10. I

HAUNTED HOTEL (page 23)

The answer is 35.

SAY BOO (page 24)

C	L	A	W		G	U	I	T	A	R		G	A	S
A	I	D	A		O	N	S	A	L	E		U	R	L
S	K	E	L	E	T	O	N	K	E	Y		A	G	E
T	E	S	L	A			T	E	A		S	N	O	W
			A	S	H	E		I	S	F	A	T		
R	I	G	H	T	O	F	F	T	H	E	B	A	T	
A	N	A	S		S	T	R		N	O	N	E	T	
G	O	R		I	S	S	U	I	N	G		A	N	O
U	R	B	A	N		I	S	O		C	M	D	R	
	G	A	V	E	U	P	T	H	E	G	H	O	S	T
	G	A	S	P	E		E	S	A	U				
P	E	E	L		S	L	O		E	T	H	E	L	
E	T	C		W	I	T	C	H	H	A	Z	E	L	S
R	N	A		O	D	E	T	T	A		P	I	S	A
K	A	N		R	E	R	O	S	E		A	R	A	T

SAY WHAT? (page 26)

"I have no Friend in the world, and from the restlessness of my destiny I never can acquire one."

SHIRLEY JACKSON H_RR_R (page 26)

Hangsaman; *The Bird's Nest*; *The Haunting of Hill House*; "The Lottery"; "The Sundial"

CONVENIENT HOUSE (page 27)

"I had the view of a castle of romance inhabited by a rosy sprite, such a place as would somehow, for diversion of the young idea, take all color out of storybooks and fairytales. Wasn't it just a storybook over which I had fallen adoze and adream? No; it was a big, ugly, antique, but convenient house, embodying a few features of a building still older, half-replaced and half-utilized, in which I had the fancy of our being almost as lost as a handful of passengers in a great drifting ship. Well, I was, strangely, at the helm!"
—Henry James, *The Turn of the Screw*

MORE GHOSTS OF LITERATURE (page 28)

1. D; 2. C; 3. E; 4. F; 5. A; 6. I; 7. J; 8. G; 9. H; 10. B

SQUARE MAZE (page 29)

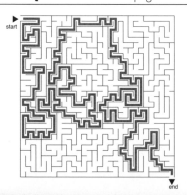

MEND THE BRIDGES (page 30)

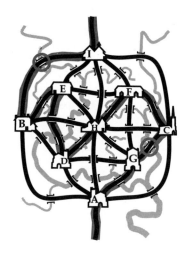

CREEPY FEARS (page 31)

1. D; 2. D; 3. B; 4. B

H_RR_R G_NR_S (page 32)

Folk; Found Footage; Gothic; Haunted House; Lovecraftian

HATRED (page 32)

"I will revenge my injuries: if I cannot inspire love, I will cause fear; and chiefly towards you my arch-enemy, because my creator, do I swear inextinguishable hatred."

—Mary Shelley, *Frankenstein*

SQUARE MAZE (page 33)

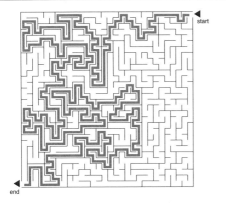

FRANKENSTEIN (page 34)

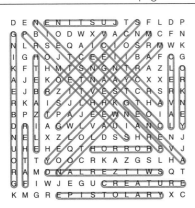

MEXICAN MONSTERS (page 36)

Tlahuelpuchi; La Llorona; Chaneque; Cipactli; Atotolin; Nagual; El Sombreron; Dtundtuncan; La Luz del Dinero; Waay Chivo

SAY WHAT? (page 36)

"There is love in me the likes of which you've never seen. There is rage in me the likes of which should never escape. If I am not satisfied in the one, I will indulge the other."

THY CREATURE (page 37)

"I am thy creature, and I will be even mild and docile to my natural lord and king, if thou wilt also perform thy part, the which thou owest me. Oh, Frankenstein, be not equitable to every other, and trample upon me alone, to whom thy justice, and even thy clemency and affection, is most due. Remember, that I am thy creature: I ought to be thy Adam; but I am rather the fallen angel, whom thou drivest from joy for no misdeed. Every where I see bliss, from which I alone am irrevocably excluded. I was benevolent and good; misery made me a fiend. Make me happy, and I shall again be virtuous."

—Mary Shelley, *Frankenstein*

ANSWER KEY

HAUNTED HOTEL (page 38)

The answer is 54.

HAUNTED CATFISH PLANTATION (PART II) (page 40)

1. C; 2. True; 3. B; 4. C

HORROR NOVELS (page 41)

1. G; 2. B; 3. J; 4. E; 5. C; 6. F; 7. H; 8. I; 9. A; 10. D

THE HAUNTED ALLEN HOUSE (page 42)

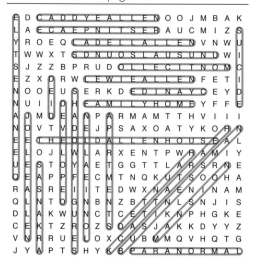

CROSSOVER MAZE (page 44)

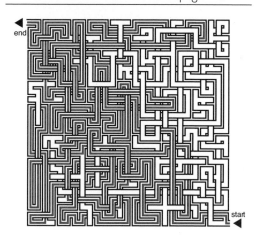

MEND THE BRIDGES (page 45)

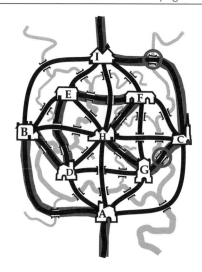

ANSWER KEY

CELTIC MONSTERS (page 46)

Abhartach; Leprechaun; Dearg Due; Selkie; Kelpie; Fomorians; Banshee; Dullahan; Sluagh; Ellen Trechend

POE ST_R__S (page 46)

"The Cask of Amontillado"; "The Gold Bug"; "The Purloined Letter"; "The Premature Burial"; "The Tell-Tale Heart"

EERIE FEARS (page 47)

1. B; 2. B; 3. D; 4. B

MORE HORROR NOVELS (page 48)

1. J; 2. A; 3. C; 4. E; 5. I; 6. G; 7. D; 8. F; 9. B; 10. H

H_RR_R G_NR_S (page 49)

Monster; Paranormal; Psychological; Science Fiction; Slasher

SPIDER (page 49)

"For where belief dwells, the spider may not stir, neither by day nor by night." —Jeremias Gotthelf, *The Black Spider*

MASTER OF SUSPENSE (page 50)

H	O	R	N		M	E	D	A	L		I	N	I	T
I	C	E	E		I	N	I	G	O		N	E	R	O
T	H	E	L	A	D	Y	V	A	N	I	S	H	E	S
S	O	D			I	R	A	E			G	N	E	I	S	S
			C	S	I			U	O	F	A			
S	P	E	L	L	B	O	U	N	D		M	A	S	S
A	R	G	U	E		S	L	I	D		H	E	T	
B	O	R	E		W	A	T	T	S		D	E	E	R
E	T	E			O	G	R	E		M	I	A	T	A
R	O	T	C		R	E	A	R	W	I	N	D	O	W
			O	D	D	S			I	D	E			
N	A	R	R	O	W		A	L	E	G		B	A	G
T	H	E	P	A	R	A	D	I	N	E	C	A	S	E
W	O	E	S		A	M	O	R	E		E	S	P	N
T	Y	K	E		P	A	G	E	R		L	E	S	T

MAD WITH LOVE (page 53)

"Then Christine gave way to fear. She trembled lest Erik should discover where Raoul was hidden; she told us in a few hurried words that Erik had gone quite mad with love and that he had decided to kill everybody and himself with everybody if she did not consent to become his wife. He had given her till eleven o'clock the next evening for reflection. It was the last respite. She must choose, as he said, between the wedding mass and the requiem."
—Gaston Leroux, *The Phantom of the Opera*

SAY WHAT? (page 52)

"I've always felt that the real horror is next door to us, that the scariest monsters are our neighbors."

EVEN MORE HORROR NOVELS (page 54)

1. G; 2. E; 3. I; 4. C; 5. A; 6. F; 7. B; 8. H; 9. D; 10. J

POE ST_R__S (page 52)

"The Black Cat"; "The Murders in the Rue Morgue"; "The Masque of the Red Death"; "The Pit and the Pendulum"; "The Oval Portrait"

SQUARE MAZE (page 55)

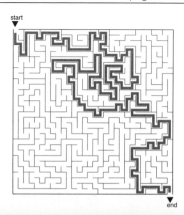

MEND THE BRIDGES (page 56)

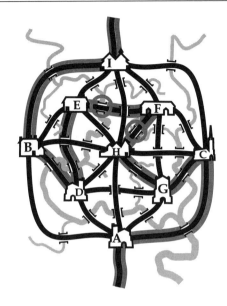

HAUNTED HOTEL (page 57)

The answer is 14.

GRUESOME FEARS (page 58)

1. C; 2. A; 3. D; 4. A

STEPHEN KING H_RR_R (page 59)

Carrie; *Pet Sematary*; *'Salem's Lot*; *The Shining*; *The Stand*

JEALOUSY (page 59)

"I am jealous of everything whose beauty does not die. I am jealous of the portrait you have painted of me. Why should it keep what I must lose?"
—Oscar Wilde, *The Picture of Dorian Gray*

WITCHES TO THE GALLOWS (page 60)

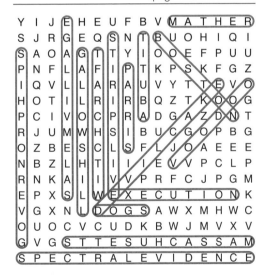

ANSWER KEY

SQUARE MAZE (page 62)

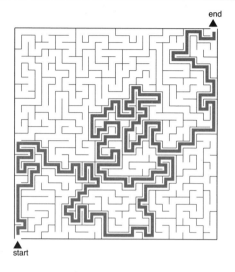

NORSE MONSTERS (page 63)

Jormungand; Huldra; Fenrir; Fafnir; Draugar; Jötnar; Grendel; Mare; Fossegrimen; Trolls

SAY WHAT? (page 63)

"At that time my virtue slumbered; my evil, kept awake by ambition, was alert and swift to seize the occasion; and the thing that was projected was Edward Hyde."

HAUNTED HOTEL (page 64)

The answer is 34.

COVER THAT FACE! (page 65)

"When at last the crowd made way for Kemp to stand erect, there lay, naked and pitiful on the ground, the bruised and broken body of a young man about thirty. His hair and brow were white—not grey with age, but white with the whiteness of albinism—and his eyes were like garnets. His hands were clenched, his eyes wide open, and his expression was one of anger and dismay. 'Cover his face' said a man. 'For Gawd's sake, cover that face!'"
—H.G. Wells, *The Invisible Man*

DOMINION (page 66)

"And Darkness and Decay and the Red Death held illimitable dominion over all."
—Edgar Allan Poe

ANSWER KEY

ALFRED HITCHCOCK H_RR_R (page 66)

Dial M for Murder; *Psycho*; *Rear Window*; *Strangers on a Train*; *The Birds*

HAUNTED HOTEL (page 67)

The answer is 18.

SLEEP PARALYSIS DEMONS (page 68)

1. I; 2. G; 3. H; 4. E; 5. B; 6. F; 7. D; 8. C; 9. J; 10. A

CIRCLE MAZE (page 69)

THE HAUNTED DR. SAMUEL A MUDD HOUSE (page 70)

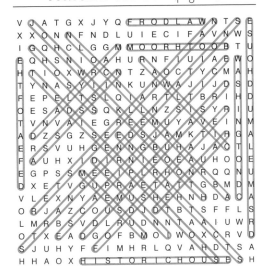

MEND THE BRIDGES (page 72)

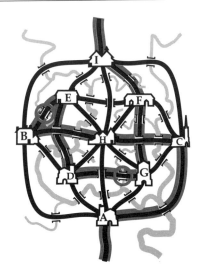

ANSWER KEY

SLAVIC MONSTERS (page 73)

Rusalka; Bannik; Balachko; Vodyanoy; Striga; Leshy; Lady Midday; Kikimora; Topielec; Vila

PETER STRAUB H_RR_R (page 73)

If You Could See Me Now; Floating Dragon; Ghost Story; Julia; Shadowland

HORRIBLE FEARS (page 74)

1. A; 2. C; 3. D; 4. D

WITCHES (page 75)

1. G; 2. E; 3. I; 4. J; 5. D; 6. A; 7. C; 8. H; 9. B; 10. F

STEPHEN KING'S BOOKS (page 76)

C	O	B	O	L	■	M	O	P	P	E	T	S
H	B	O	■	I	S	A	W	■	E	L	I	A
R	I	D	D	A	N	C	E	■	T	M	A	N
I	■	O	R	I	E	N	T	S	■	R	■	
S	P	E	C	■	P	■	B	E	T	A	S	
T	I	L	T	■	P	A	N	A	M	A	■	A
I	N	T	O	N	E	■	U	R	A	C	I	L
N	■	O	R	A	T	O	R	■	T	I	D	E
E	R	N	S	T	■	T	■	A	T	O	M	
■	O	■	L	E	A	G	U	E	R	■	S	
C	U	B	E	■	C	A	R	R	Y	A	L	L
A	G	U	E	■	U	T	E	S	■	B	I	O
D	E	S	P	I	T	E	■	E	X	U	L	T

HAUNTED HOTEL (page 78)

The answer is 42.

ANSWER KEY

SAY WHAT? (page 79)

"The vacant mind is ever on the watch for relief, and ready to plunge into error, to escape from the languor of idleness."

STEPHEN KING H_RR_R (page 79)

Bag of Bones; *Black House*; *Doctor Sleep*; *Desperation*; *Misery*

PALLID MASK (page 80)

"This is the thing that troubles me, for I cannot forget Carcosa where black stars hang in the heavens; where the shadows of men's thoughts lengthen in the afternoon, when the twin suns sink into the lake of Hali; and my mind will bear for ever the memory of the Pallid Mask. I pray God will curse the writer, as the writer has cursed the world with this beautiful, stupendous creation, terrible in its simplicity, irresistible in its truth—a world which now trembles before the King in Yellow."
—Robert W. Chambers, *The King in Yellow*

HAUNTED HOUSES OF LITERATURE (page 81)

1. E; 2. D; 3. C; 4. A; 5. H; 6. B; 7. I; 8. F; 9. G; 10. J

SCARY HALLOWEEN (page 82)

MEND THE BRIDGES (page 84)

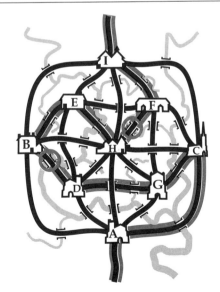

ANSWER KEY

MONSTROUS FEARS (page 85)

1. A; 2. D; 3. C; 4. A

DAVID CRONENBERG H_RR_R
(page 86)

Dead Ringers; *The Brood*; *The Dead Zone*; *The Fly*; *Videodrome*

MASK (page 86)

"The mask of self-deception was no longer a mask for me, it was a part of me." —Robert W. Chambers, *The King in Yellow*

SQUARE MAZE (page 87)

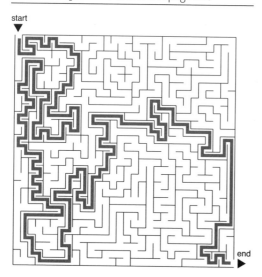

MYTHICAL CREATURES (page 88)

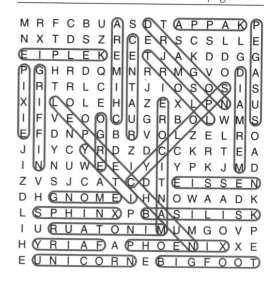

GREEK MONSTERS (page 90)

Charybdis; Manticore; Cerberus; Hydra; Chimera; Hippocampus; Minotaur; Gorgon; Typhon; Siren

ANSWER KEY

SAY WHAT? (page 90)

"Welcome to my house. Come freely. Go safely; and leave something of the happiness you bring!"

SUPERSTITION (page 91)

"The superstition upon which this tale is founded is very general in the East. Among the Arabians it appears to be common: it did not, however, extend itself to the Greeks until after the establishment of Christianity; and it has only assumed its present form since the division of the Latin and Greek churches; at which time, the idea becoming prevalent, that a Latin body could not corrupt if buried in their territory, it gradually increased, and formed the subject of many wonderful stories, still extant, of the dead rising from their graves, and feeding upon the blood of the young and beautiful."
—John William Polidori, "The Vampyre"

HAUNTED HOTEL (page 92)

The answer is 37.

HAUNTED HOTEL PROVINCIAL (PART II) (page 94)

1. False; 2. A; 3. False; 4. D

VAMPIRES OF LITERATURE (page 95)

1. G; 2. B; 3. I; 4. F; 5. D; 6. E; 7. A; 8. J; 9. C; 10. H

THE HAUNTED ST. ELMO GHOST TOWN (page 96)

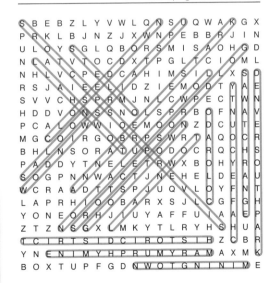

CROSSOVER MAZE (page 98)

MEND THE BRIDGES (page 99)

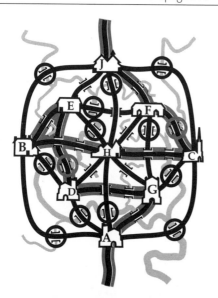

WEST AFRICAN MONSTERS (page 100)

Obia; Kongamato; Ninki Nanka; Abonsam; Ogbanje; Azde; Hira; Obayifo; Mokele-mbembe; Emela-ntouka

ANNE RICE H_RR_R (page 100)

Lasher; Interview with the Vampire; The Queen of the Damned; The Vampire Lestat; The Witching Hour

NIGHTMARISH FEARS (page 101)

1. C; 2. A; 3. B; 4. D

HAUNTED PLACES (page 102)

1. B; 2. D; 3. A; 4. C; 5. H; 6. G; 7. J; 8. I; 9. F; 10. E

ANSWER KEY

HAUNTED HOTEL (page 103)

The answer is 35.

SCARY MONSTERS (page 104)

C	H	A	R	T	R	E	S		C	L	A	W
L	U	S	H		I	S	P		H	O	N	E
O	T	T	O		N	P	R		I	C	O	N
G	U	A	M		G	I	A		C	H	A	T
		B	O	G	E	Y	M	A	N			
A	R	F		F	I	D		E	G	E	S	T
B	E	R	E	F	T		D	R	O	S	S	Y
S	P	I	R	E		T	R	Y		S	H	R
	G	A	R	G	O	Y	L	E				
B	A	H	S		A	W	N		S	A	S	S
A	L	T	I		M	A	E		T	R	I	O
B	I	E	N		M	R	S		E	A	R	L
S	A	N	G		A	D	S	O	R	B	E	D

SAY WHAT? (page 106)

"He who wins a thousand common hearts, is therefore entitled to some renown; but he who keeps undisputed sway over the heart of a coquette, is indeed a hero."

GUILLERMO DEL TORO H_RR_R (page 106)

Crimson Peak; Cronos; Mimic; Pan's Labyrinth; The Devil's Backbone

MONSTROUS LAWS (page 107)

"We are punished for our refusals. Every impulse that we strive to strangle broods in the mind and poisons us. The body sins once, and has done with its sin, for action is a mode of purification. Nothing remains then but the recollection of a pleasure, or the luxury of a regret. The only way to get rid of a temptation is to yield to it. Resist it, and your soul grows sick with longing for the things it has forbidden to itself, with desire for what its monstrous laws have made monstrous and unlawful."
—Oscar Wilde, *The Picture of Dorian Gray*

MORE HAUNTED PLACES (page 108)

1. B; 2. J; 3. F; 4. C; 5. E; 6. A; 7. G; 8. I; 9. H; 10. D

SQUARE MAZE (page 109)

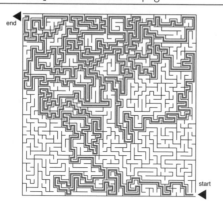

MEND THE BRIDGES (page 110)

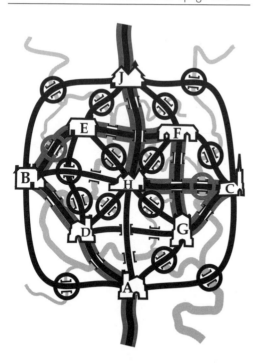

HAUNTED HOTEL (page 111)

The answer is 17.

OUTRAGEOUS FEARS (page 112)

1. C; 2. B; 3. B; 4. A

SHADOWY BOUNDARIES (page 113)

"The boundaries which divide Life from Death are at best shadowy and vague. Who shall say where the one ends, and where the other begins?"
—Edgar Allan Poe

H_RR_R G_NR_S (page 113)

Supernatural; Survival; Vampire; Witchcraft; Zombie

EDGAR ALLAN POE (page 114)

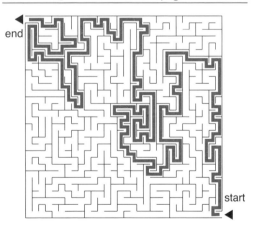

```
R H  P  I D H T A E D D E R X T A G G M
E S  O  I A O F R K W E L T I H O A L K
T Y  E  W I X I B D K T W P R T G W U X
I R  E  T H E T E L L T A L E H E A R T T
R U  R  I S A V I R G I N I A C L E M M
W R  Y  J W Z F E R B A C A M O Y L A X
E E  L  L E B A N N A X M A Y D M E L J
E K  O  J F H X Y K S C N U U L Q N H C
N A  N  E L E H O T I M M V L U X O E W
A L  R  O M A N T I C I S M I C U X R K
L R  V  G P U R L O I N E D Y K H A E Y
E Q  P  N O I T C I F E V I T C E T E D
M Q  P  O F M P E H D T S J F T S Q N P
A U  O  W A U Y H O U S E O F U S H E R
T T  Y  S L U C R Y P T O G R A P H Y B
S A  Q  R A R J H T I N E V E R M O R E
A U  U  K Y Q A M O N T I L L A D O E R
E A  R  T H U R G O R D O N P Y M Y S I
```

SQUARE MAZE (page 116)

end ◄

start ►

SAY WHAT? (page 117)

"I have never met a vampire personally, but I don't know what might happen tomorrow."

INDIAN MONSTERS (page 117)

Bhoota; Pishacha; Bhoota Vahana Yantra; Rakshasa; Penchapenchi; Yakshini; Tekhumiavi; Nishi; Kirtimukha; Preta

A FIGURE ON HORSEBACK (page 118)

"The dominant spirit, however, that haunts this enchanted region, and seems to be commander-in-chief of all the powers of the air, is the apparition of a figure on horseback, without a head. It is said by some to be the ghost of a Hessian trooper, whose head had been carried away by a cannon-ball, in some nameless battle during the Revolutionary War, and who is ever and anon seen by the country folk hurrying along in the gloom of night, as if on the wings of the wind."
—Washington Irving, "The Legend of Sleepy Hollow"

YALE'S SPIRITED ORGANIST (PART II) (page 120)

1. A; 2. B; 3. B; 4. True

ANSWER KEY

HAUNTED HOTEL (page 121)

The answer is 48.

HORROR MOVIE ICONS (page 122)

1. H; 2. J; 3. D; 4. G; 5. I; 6. F; 7. C;
8. B; 9. E; 10. A

JOHN CARPENTER
H_RR_R (page 123)

*Halloween; In the Mouth of Madness;
Prince of Darkness; The Fog; The Thing*

ALONE (page 123)

"He rarely went abroad by daylight, but
at twilight he would go out muffled up
invisibly, whether the weather were cold
or not, and he chose the loneliest paths
and those most overshadowed by trees
and banks."
—H.G. Wells, *The Invisible Man*

THE HAUNTED GARNET
GHOST TOWN (page 124)

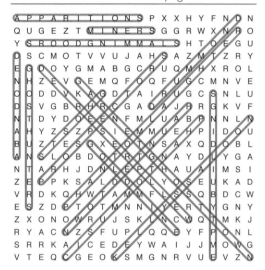

MEND THE BRIDGES (page 126)

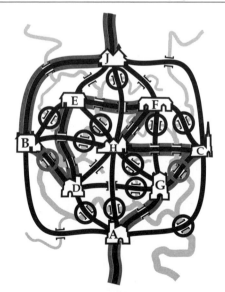

ANSWER KEY

JAPANESE MONSTERS (page 127)

Nurikabe; Nure-onna; Kamaitachi; Obariyon; Gashadokuro; Oni; Chimimouryou; Jorogumo; Tsukumogami; Kitsune

SAM RAIMI H_RR_R (page 127)

Drag Me to Hell; *Darkman*; *Army of Darkness*; *The Gift*; *The Evil Dead*

PETRIFYING FEARS (page 128)

1. C; 2. B; 3. A; 4. A

MORE HORROR MOVIE ICONS (page 129)

1. F; 2. D; 3. I; 4. B; 5. J; 6. A; 7. C; 8. E; 9. H; 10. G

THINGS THAT GO BUMP IN THE NIGHT (page 130)

```
 H  O  O  T  ██  A  C  T  O  R
 O  R  T  H  ██  L  A  I  L  A
 W  E  R  E  W  O  L  V  E  S
 L  O  O  R  A  ██  C  O  S  I
 ██ ██  A  S  E  ██  L  O  N
 S  W  A  M  P  T  H  I  N  G
 C  A  R  ██  S  A  O  ██
 A  S  I  A  ██  T  T  O  P  S
 G  H  O  S  T  S  T  O  R  Y
 G  U  S  T  S  ██  U  L  A  N
 S  P  O  O  K  ██  B  A  T  S
```

HAUNTED HOTEL (page 132)

The answer is 35.

SAY WHAT? (page 133)

"Yes, Dorian, you will always be fond of me. I represent to you all the sins you never had the courage to commit."

DARIO ARGENTO
H_RR_R (page 133)

Deep Red; Inferno; Phenomena; Suspiria; The Mother of Tears

UNEQUAL BARGAIN (page 134)

"To cast in my lot with Jekyll, was to die to those appetites which I had long secretly indulged and had of late begun to pamper. To cast it in with Hyde, was to die to a thousand interests and aspirations, and to become, at a blow and forever, despised and friendless. The bargain might appear unequal; but there was still another consideration in the scales; for while Jekyll would suffer smartingly in the fires of abstinence, Hyde would be not even conscious of all that he had lost."
—Robert Louis Stevenson, *The Strange Case of Dr. Jekyll and Mr. Hyde*

VAMPIRIC MONSTERS (page 135)

1. C; 2. I; 3. A; 4. F; 5. E; 6. D; 7. B; 8. J; 9. H; 10. G

CIRCLE MAZE (page 136)

MEND THE BRIDGES (page 137)

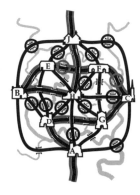

SPINE-CHILLING FEARS (page 138)

1. A; 2. D; 3. D; 4. D

MIKE FLANAGAN
H_RR_R (page 139)

Midnight Mass; The Fall of the House of Usher; The Haunting of Bly Manor; The Haunting of Hill House; The Midnight Club

SEA OF WONDERS (page 139)

"I am all in a sea of wonders. I doubt;
I fear; I think strange things, which
I dare not confess to my own soul.
God keep me, if only for the sake of
those dear to me!"
—Bram Stoker, *Dracula*

DRACULA (page 140)

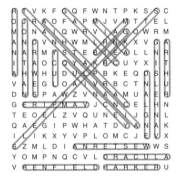

SQUARE MAZE (page 142)

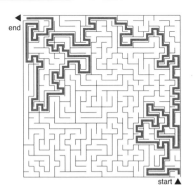

INDONESIAN MONSTERS (page 143)

Banaspati; Penanggalan; Orang bunian;
Babi ngepet; Pocong; Rangda; Leyak;
Nyi Blorong; Ahool; Buto Ijo; Kuntilanak

SAY WHAT? (page 143)

"There comes an end to all things; the
most capacious measure is filled at last;
and this brief condescension to evil
finally destroyed the balance of my soul."

CLEVER MAN (page 144)

"You are clever man, friend John; you
reason well, and your wit is bold; but
you are too prejudiced. You do not let
your eyes see nor your ears hear, and
that which is outside your daily life
is not of account to you. Do you not
think that there are things which you
cannot understand, and yet which are;
that some people see things that others
cannot? But there are things old and
new which must not be contemplate by
men's eyes, because they know—or think
they know—some things which other
men have told them."
—Bram Stoker, *Dracula*

CROSSOVER MAZE (page 145)

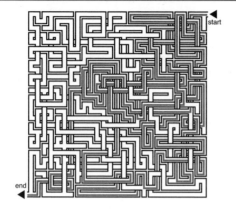

WES CRAVEN H_RR_R (page 146)

A Nightmare on Elm Street; New Nightmare; Scream; The Hills Have Eyes; The People Under the Stairs

CRUEL LOVE (page 146)

"You will think me cruel, very selfish, but love is always selfish; the more ardent the more selfish."
—Joseph Sheridan Le Fanu, *Carmilla*

HAUNTED HOTEL (page 147)

The answer is 15.

HORROR GAMES (page 148)

1. I; 2. A; 3. F; 4. C; 5. G; 6. B; 7. D; 8. H; 9. E; 10. J

PETER STRAUB H_RR_R (page 149)

A Dark Matter; Koko; Lost Boy Lost Girl; In the Night Room; The Talisman

THIS LITTLE VALLEY (page 149)

"If ever I should wish for a retreat whither I might steal from the world and its distractions, and dream quietly away the remnant of a troubled life, I know of none more promising than this little valley."
—Washington Irving, "The Legend of Sleepy Hollow"

ANSWER KEY

HAUNTINGS IN CONNECTICUT (page 150)

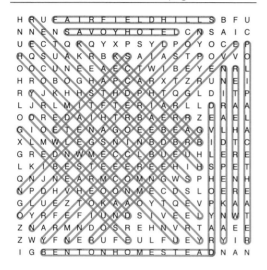

MEND THE BRIDGES (page 152)

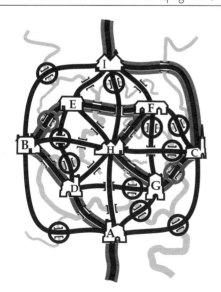

AUSTRALIAN MONSTERS (page 153)

Yara-ma-yha-who; Hoop snake; Drop bear; Rainbow serpent; Bunyip; Tiddalik; Muldjewangk; Burrunjor; Blue mountains panther; Hawkesbury river monster

JAMES WAN H_RR_R (page 153)

Dead Silence; *Malignant*; *Insidious*; *Saw*; *The Conjuring*

TERRIFYING FEARS (page 154)

1. B; 2. A; 3. B; 4. B

MORE HORROR GAMES (page 155)

1. F; 2. C; 3. J; 4. I; 5. E; 6. B; 7. H; 8. A; 9. D; 10. G

DRACULA (page 156)

HAUNTED HOTEL (page 158)

The answer is 36.

ANSWER KEY

SAY WHAT? (page 159)

"The fallen angel becomes a malignant devil. Yet even that enemy of God and man had friends and associates in his desolation; I am alone."

M. NIGHT SHYAMALAN H_RR_R (page 159)

Knock at the Cabin; *Signs*; *Split*; *The Sixth Sense*; *The Village*

TRANSPARENT (page 160)

"You may well exclaim. I remember that night. It was late at night—in the daytime one was bothered with the gaping, silly students—and I worked then sometimes till dawn. It came suddenly, splendid and complete in my mind. I was alone; the laboratory was still, with the tall lights burning brightly and silently. In all my great moments I have been alone. 'One could make an animal—a tissue—transparent! One could make it invisible! All except the pigments—I could be invisible!' I said, suddenly realising what it meant to be an albino with such knowledge. It was overwhelming."
—H.G. Wells, *The Invisible Man*

TOP TEN HORROR FILMS (page 161)

1. H; 2. B; 3. E; 4. G; 5. J; 6. A; 7. D; 8. F; 9. I; 10. C

THE HAUNTED WINCHESTER MYSTERY HOUSE (page 162)

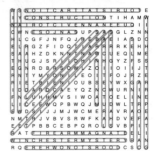

SQUARE MAZE (page 164)

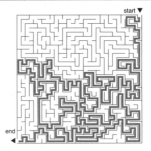

MEND THE BRIDGES (page 165)

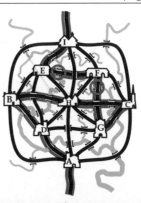